FAVORITE BRAND NAME

Great VEGETARIAN Meals

Easy • Delicious • Nutritious

Publications International, Ltd.

Pictured on the front cover: Broccoli-Tofu Stir-Fry *(page 86)*.
Pictured on the back cover *(clockwise from top right):* Artichoke Heart, Olive and Goat Cheese Pizza *(page 20),* Broccoli Lasagna Bianca *(page 66),* Rice Cakes with Mushroom Walnut Ragoût *(page 84)* and Cool Italian Tomato Soup *(page 18).*

ISBN: 0-7853-2233-7

Manufactured in U.S.A.

8 7 6 5 4 3 2 1

Microwave Cooking: Microwave ovens vary in wattage. The microwave cooking times given in this publication are approximate. Use the cooking times as guidelines and check for doneness before adding more time. Consult manufacturer's instructions for suitable microwave-safe cooking dishes.

Introduction 6

Satisfying Soups & Salads 8

Pizzas & Sandwiches 20

Enticing Eggs & Cheese 30

Grains & Beans 40

Family-Pleasing Pastas 56

Main Dishes 74

Acknowledgments 90

Index 91

FAVORITE BRAND NAME

Great VEGETARIAN Meals

Easy • *Delicious* • *Nutritious*

Vegetarian Cooking

The latest guidelines from the United States Department of Agriculture and the Department of Health and Human Services suggest that a healthful diet should include lots of grain-based foods, fruits and vegetables. These organizations and registered dietitians recommend reducing the consumption of animal-based foods in order to reduce total fat, saturated fat and cholesterol in our diets. One way to do that is to add more vegetarian dishes to every-day meals. In fact, many nonvegetarians are choosing to eat meatless meals several times a week. In the process, they are discovering what vegetarians have known for a long time--plant foods, such as grains, fruits and vegetables, can be a satisfying alternative to animal-based foods and are generally lower in cost than meat, poultry and seafood.

HELPFUL HINTS

• Grains have been food staples for years because they offer an inexpensive source of low-fat protein. They are high in complex carbohydrates, providing the body with a steady supply of energy. Add rice, barley, corn and wild rice to soups, salads and entrées to increase the nutritional value of any meal.

• Pasta is a wise selection for meatless meals. It is an excellent source of low-fat complex carbohydrates and provides a good supply of iron, magnesium, thiamin, niacin and riboflavin. Pair it with a tasty sauce and plenty of vegetables.

• Take advantage of the vast array of breads that are readily available. Choose from packaged loaves, bakery loaves, pita breads and tortillas. Whole-grain breads, which are higher in fiber and protein, are a wise choice. Easy to make quick breads add a tasty touch to a meal.

• Dried beans are an inexpensive high-protein, low-sodium alternative to meats in chilis, soups, salads, burritos and enchiladas. Beans are high in complex carbohydrates, the major source of energy in the human diet. They are also low in fat, cholesterol free and high in fiber.

• Tofu is a high-protein substitute for animal-based foods. Made from soybeans, it is cholesterol free, low in saturated fat and a good source of calcium. Tofu's bland flavor readily takes on the flavor of other foods, making it the perfect addition to stir-fries and other entrées.

MEATLESS MENUS

Spring Brunch

Papaya-Kiwifruit Salad with Orange
Dressing (page 15)
Asparagus-Swiss Soufflé (page 32)
assorted muffins and scones

Spring in the Park

Cool Italian Tomato Soup (page 18)
Black Bean-and-Barley Salad (page 44)
Meatless Muffaletta Sandwich
(page 26)
fresh berries

Football Tailgate Party

Chunky Vegetable Chili (page 13)
corn bread
Texas Onion Pepper Tart (page 32)
brownies and cookies

Italian Supper

Tuscan Summer Salad (page 18)
Eggplant Crêpes with Roasted Tomato
Sauce (page 79)
biscotti

Middle Eastern Lunch

hummus with assorted crudités
Tabbouleh (page 48)
Spinach & Tomato Tofu Toss (page 29)
baklava

Elegant Fall Dinner Party

Cream of Pumpkin Curry Soup (page 18)
Winter Pear and Stilton Salad (page 8)
Rice Cakes with Mushroom Walnut
Ragoût (page 84)
apple tart

• Add more vegetables to your diet by including them in appetizers, salads, sandwiches, soups and entrées. They are low in fat and rich in vitamins. For more fiber, enjoy vegetables raw as a snack.

• Fruit provides the sweetness many of us crave without a lot of fat or calories, making it an ideal snack. It's easy to include it in every meal—it makes an interesting addition to salads, grain dishes and entrées, and a succulent dessert.

• Eggs and cheese are great sources of protein. If you are trying to reduce fat and cholesterol, simply substitute reduced-fat products for cheese and sour cream and cholesterol-free eggs substitutes or egg whites for whole eggs.

• If some family members decide that meatless meals are not for them, serve them a small portion of lean meat, poultry or seafood along with the vegetarian recipe.

Satisfying Soups & Salads

Winter Pear and Stilton Salad

⅓ cup extra virgin olive oil
1½ tablespoons sherry wine vinegar or
    white wine vinegar
1 tablespoon Dijon mustard
4 teaspoons honey
¼ teaspoon salt
5 cups packed torn assorted gourmet
    mixed salad greens, such as
    oakleaf, frisee, watercress,
    radicchio, arugula or escarole
    (about 3 ounces)
2 cups packed torn Boston or Bibb
    lettuce leaves (about 1½ ounces)
2 ripe Bosc, Bartlett or Anjou pears,
    cored, quartered and cut into
    ½-inch pieces
    Lemon juice
1½ cups (6 ounces) crumbled Stilton or
    Gorgonzola cheese
    Freshly ground black pepper

Place oil, vinegar, mustard, honey and salt in small bowl. Whisk until combined. Cover and refrigerate up to 2 days.

Combine all salad greens in large bowl. To help prevent discoloration, brush pear pieces with lemon juice, if desired. Add pears, cheese and dressing to salad mixture. Toss lightly to coat; sprinkle with pepper.

Makes 6 to 8 servings

Thai Pasta Salad with Peanut Sauce

¼ cup evaporated skim milk
4½ teaspoons creamy peanut butter
4½ teaspoons finely chopped red onion
1 teaspoon lemon juice
¾ teaspoon brown sugar
½ teaspoon reduced-sodium soy sauce
⅛ teaspoon crushed red pepper
½ teaspoon finely chopped fresh ginger
1 cup hot cooked whole wheat spaghetti
2 teaspoons finely chopped green onion

1. Combine milk, peanut butter, red onion, lemon juice, sugar, soy sauce and red pepper in medium saucepan. Bring to a boil over high heat, stirring constantly. Boil 2 minutes, stirring constantly. Reduce heat to medium-low. Add ginger; blend well. Add spaghetti; toss to coat.

2. Top servings evenly with green onion. Serve immediately.   *Makes 2 servings*

Winter Pear and Stilton Salad

Greens, White Bean and Barley Soup

½ pound carrots, peeled
2 tablespoons olive oil
1½ cups chopped onions
2 cloves garlic, minced
1½ cups sliced button mushrooms
6 cups Vegetable Stock (page 16)
2 cups cooked barley
1 can (16 ounces) Great Northern beans, drained and rinsed
2 bay leaves
1 teaspoon sugar
1 teaspoon dried thyme leaves
1½ pounds collard greens, washed, stemmed and chopped (about 7 cups)
1 tablespoon white wine vinegar
Hot pepper sauce
Red bell pepper strips for garnish

Cut carrots lengthwise into quarters; cut crosswise into ¼-inch pieces. Heat oil in Dutch oven over medium heat until hot. Add carrots, onions and garlic; cook and stir 3 minutes. Add mushrooms; cook and stir 5 minutes or until tender.

Add stock, barley, beans, bay leaves, sugar and thyme. Bring to a boil over high heat. Reduce heat to low. Cover and simmer 5 minutes. Add greens; simmer 10 minutes. Remove bay leaves; discard. Stir in vinegar. Season to taste with pepper sauce. Garnish, if desired. *Makes 8 servings*

Roasted Winter Vegetable Soup

1 small or ½ medium acorn squash, halved
2 medium tomatoes
1 medium onion, unpeeled
1 green bell pepper, halved
1 red bell pepper, halved
2 small red potatoes
3 cloves garlic, unpeeled
1½ cups tomato juice
½ cup water
4 teaspoons vegetable oil
1 tablespoon red wine vinegar
¼ teaspoon ground black pepper
¾ cup chopped fresh cilantro
4 tablespoons nonfat sour cream

1. Preheat oven to 400°F. Spray baking sheet with nonstick cooking spray. Place acorn squash, tomatoes, onion, bell peppers, potatoes and garlic on baking sheet. Bake 40 minutes, removing garlic and tomatoes after 10 minutes. Let stand 15 minutes or until cool enough to handle.

2. Peel vegetables and garlic; discard skins. Coarsely chop vegetables. Combine half of chopped vegetables, tomato juice, ½ cup water, oil and vinegar in food processor or blender; process until smooth.

3. Combine puréed vegetables, remaining chopped vegetables and black pepper in large saucepan. Bring to a simmer over medium-high heat. Simmer 5 minutes or until heated through, stirring constantly. Top servings evenly with cilantro and sour cream. *Makes 4 servings*

Greens, White Bean and Barley Soup

Easy Greek Salad

Easy Greek Salad

6 leaves romaine lettuce, washed and
    torn into 1½-inch pieces
1 cucumber, peeled and sliced
1 tomato, chopped
½ cup sliced red onion
1 ounce feta cheese, crumbled (about
    ⅓ cup)
2 tablespoons extra-virgin olive oil
2 tablespoons lemon juice
1 teaspoon dried oregano leaves
½ teaspoon salt

1. Combine lettuce, cucumber, tomato, onion
and cheese in large serving bowl.

2. Whisk together oil, lemon juice, oregano
and salt in small bowl. Pour over lettuce
mixture; toss until coated. Serve
immediately.   *Makes 6 servings*

Curried Wild Rice Soup

1 medium onion, chopped
¼ cup butter or margarine
2½ cups sliced fresh mushrooms
½ cup chopped celery
½ cup all-purpose flour
6 cups vegetable broth
2 cups cooked California Wild Rice
2 cups half-and-half
⅔ cup dry sherry
½ teaspoon salt
½ teaspoon white pepper
½ teaspoon (or more) curry powder
½ teaspoon dry mustard
½ teaspoon paprika
½ teaspoon dried chervil
    Parsley or chives, chopped

Sauté onion in butter in large saucepan until golden brown. Add mushrooms and celery. Cook 2 minutes, stirring constantly. Stir in flour; cook over low heat, stirring until mixture is bubbly. Gradually add broth. Heat to a boil, stirring constantly. Boil and stir 1 minute. Add wild rice, half-and-half, sherry and seasonings; heat to a simmer. Garnish with parsley. *Makes 12 servings*

Favorite recipe from **California Wild Rice**

Chunky Vegetable Chili

2 tablespoons vegetable oil
1 medium onion, chopped
2 ribs celery, diced
1 carrot, diced
3 cloves garlic, minced
2 cans (about 15 ounces each) Great Northern beans, rinsed and drained
1½ cups water
1 cup frozen corn
1 can (6 ounces) tomato paste
1 can (4 ounces) diced mild green chilies, undrained
1 tablespoon chili powder
2 teaspoons dried oregano leaves
1 teaspoon salt

1. Heat oil in large skillet over medium-high heat until hot. Add onion, celery, carrot and garlic; cook 5 minutes or until vegetables are tender, stirring occasionally.

2. Stir beans, 1½ cups water, corn, tomato paste, chilies, chili powder, oregano and salt into skillet. Reduce heat to medium-low. Simmer 20 minutes, stirring occasionally. Garnish with cilantro, if desired.
Makes 8 servings

Warm Mushroom Salad

2 quarts mixed salad greens (such as spinach, arugula, curly endive and romaine)
3 tablespoons FILIPPO BERIO® Olive Oil
1 (10-ounce) package mushrooms, cleaned and quartered or sliced
3 shallots, chopped
1 clove garlic, crushed
2 tablespoons chopped fresh chives
2 tablespoons lemon juice
2 tablespoons balsamic vinegar
1 teaspoon sugar
1½ cups purchased garlic croutons
Shavings of Parmesan cheese
Salt and freshly ground black pepper

Tear salad greens into bite-size pieces. Arrange on 4 serving plates. In medium skillet, heat olive oil over medium heat until hot. Add mushrooms, shallots and garlic; cook and stir 3 to 5 minutes or until mushrooms are softened. Stir in chives, lemon juice, vinegar and sugar; simmer 30 seconds. Spoon mixture over salad greens. Top with croutons and Parmesan cheese. Season to taste with salt and pepper.
Makes 4 to 6 servings

Papaya-Kiwifruit Salad with Orange Dressing

1 papaya
4 kiwifruit
6 tablespoons frozen orange juice
    concentrate, thawed
3 tablespoons honey
1 cup sour cream
1 tablespoon grated orange peel
1 tablespoon grated lime peel

1. Peel and remove seeds from papaya. Slice lengthwise into thin slices.

2. Peel kiwifruit and cut crosswise into thin slices. Arrange papaya and kiwifruit on 4 salad plates.

3. Combine orange juice concentrate and honey in small bowl. Stir in sour cream. Spoon dressing over salads; sprinkle with peels. *Makes 4 servings*

Hearty Vegetable Gumbo

    Nonstick cooking spray
½ cup chopped onion
½ cup chopped green bell pepper
¼ cup chopped celery
2 cloves garlic, minced
2 cans (about 14 ounces each) no-salt-
    added stewed tomatoes, undrained
2 cups no-salt-added tomato juice
1 can (15 ounces) red beans, drained
    and rinsed
1 tablespoon chopped fresh parsley
¼ teaspoon dried oregano leaves
¼ teaspoon hot pepper sauce
2 bay leaves
1½ cups quick-cooking brown rice
1 package (10 ounces) frozen chopped
    okra, thawed

1. Spray 4-quart Dutch oven with cooking spray; heat over medium heat until hot. Add onion, bell pepper, celery and garlic. Cook and stir 3 minutes or until crisp-tender.

2. Add stewed tomatoes, juice, beans, parsley, oregano, pepper sauce and bay leaves. Bring to a boil over high heat. Add rice. Reduce heat to medium-low. Simmer, covered, 15 minutes or until rice is tender.

3. Add okra; simmer, covered, 5 minutes more or until okra is tender. Remove bay leaves; discard. Garnish as desired.
Makes 4 (2-cup) servings

Spinach and Strawberry Salad with Wisconsin Gouda

¼ cup orange juice
3 tablespoons vegetable oil
1 tablespoon honey
1 teaspoon grated orange peel
¼ teaspoon garlic salt
⅛ teaspoon paprika
4 cups spinach leaves
1 pint strawberries, stemmed and
    halved
1 cup (4 ounces) Wisconsin Gouda
    Cheese, cubed
½ cup pecan or walnut halves

Combine orange juice, oil, honey, orange peel, garlic salt and paprika in small container with tight lid; shake well.

Toss spinach leaves, strawberries, cheese and nuts with dressing in large salad bowl. Refrigerate or serve immediately.
Makes 6 servings

Favorite recipe from **Wisconsin Milk Marketing Board**

Hearty Vegetable Gumbo

Chilled Potato Cucumber Soup with Roasted Red Pepper Swirl

1 large cucumber, peeled and seeded
1½ cups canned vegetable broth
1 cup chopped leeks
1 cup cubed, peeled red potatoes
1 cup water
1 teaspoon ground cumin
1 cup buttermilk
½ teaspoon salt
¼ teaspoon ground white pepper
    Red Pepper Swirl (recipe follows)
    Fresh chives for garnish

Cut cucumber halves into quarters; cut crosswise into ½-inch pieces. Combine cucumber, broth, leeks, potatoes, water and cumin in large saucepan. Bring to a boil over high heat. Reduce heat to low. Cover and simmer 20 minutes or until vegetables are tender. Cool.

Process cucumber mixture in food processor in batches until smooth. Pour into large bowl. Stir in buttermilk, salt and pepper. Cover; refrigerate until cold.

Just before serving, prepare Roasted Red Pepper Swirl. Ladle soup into bowls; spoon Roasted Red Pepper Swirl into soup and swirl with knife. Garnish, if desired.

Makes 6 servings

Roasted Red Pepper Swirl

3 cups diced red bell peppers
1 small dried hot red chili, seeded and
    torn
½ cup boiling water
1 clove garlic, sliced
2 teaspoons white wine vinegar

Preheat oven to 400°F. Spray nonstick baking sheet with cooking spray. Place bell peppers and chili on prepared baking sheet.

Bake 30 minutes or until bell pepper is browned on edges, stirring after 15 minutes. Process peppers, chili, boiling water, garlic and vinegar in food processor until smooth.

Makes ¾ cup

Vegetable Stock

2 medium onions
2 tablespoons vegetable oil
2 leeks, cleaned
3 ribs celery, cut into 2-inch pieces
8 cups cold water
6 medium carrots, cut into 1-inch
    pieces
1 turnip, peeled, cut into chunks
    (optional)
2 cloves garlic, peeled and crushed
4 parsley sprigs
1 teaspoon dried thyme leaves, crushed
¼ teaspoon ground black pepper
2 bay leaves

Trim tops and roots from onions, leaving most of dried outer skin intact; cut into wedges.

Heat oil in stockpot or 5-quart Dutch oven over medium-high heat until hot. Add onions, leeks and celery; cook and stir 5 minutes or until vegetables are limp but not brown. Add water, carrots, turnip, garlic, parsley, thyme, pepper and bay leaves. Bring to a boil over high heat. Reduce heat to medium-low; simmer, uncovered, 1½ hours. Remove from heat. Cool slightly and strain through large sieve or colander to remove vegetables. Press vegetables lightly with slotted spoon to remove excess liquid; discard vegetables.

Use immediately or refrigerate stock in tightly covered container up to 2 days or freeze stock in batches in freezer containers for several months.

Makes about 7 cups stock

Tortellini Asparagus Salad

1 pound fresh asparagus, cut into
    ½-inch pieces
2 cups tightly packed fresh spinach
    leaves, torn into bite-sized pieces
1 cup diced red bell pepper
2 packages (9 ounces each) small
    cheese-filled tortellini, cooked,
    drained, cooled
¼ cup red wine vinegar
2 tablespoons olive or vegetable oil
1½ teaspoons lemon juice
1 teaspoon sugar
1 teaspoon LAWRY'S® Garlic Salt

Place asparagus on steamer rack; place in deep pot with 1-inch boiling water. Cover and steam 10 minutes. Remove and set aside. Steam spinach on steamer rack in same pot about 45 seconds or until just wilted. In large bowl, combine asparagus, spinach, red pepper and tortellini; blend well. In small bowl, combine vinegar, oil, lemon juice, sugar and Garlic Salt; blend well. Pour over tortellini mixture; toss well.

Makes 4 servings

Hints: Substitute 1½ cups broccoli florets for asparagus. Chopped pimientos can be substituted for red bell pepper.

Tortellini Asparagus Salad

Cool Italian Tomato Soup

1¾ cups (14.5-ounce can) CONTADINA®
    Pasta Ready Chunky Tomatoes
    with Crushed Red Pepper,
    undrained
2 cups tomato juice
½ cup half-and-half
2 tablespoons lemon juice
1 large cucumber, peeled, diced (about
    2 cups)
1 medium green bell pepper, diced
    (about ½ cup)
    Chopped fresh basil (optional)
    Croutons (optional)

In blender container, place tomatoes with juice, tomato juice, half-and-half and lemon juice; blend until smooth. Pour into large bowl or soup tureen; stir in cucumber and bell pepper. Sprinkle with basil and croutons just before serving, if desired.

Makes 6 servings

Tuscan Summer Salad

1 small loaf coarse day-old Italian
    bread
¼ cup olive oil
3 tablespoons balsamic vinegar
1 clove garlic, crushed
1 teaspoon salt
1 teaspoon TABASCO® pepper sauce
3 large ripe tomatoes, cut into large
    chunks
1 large red onion, cut in half and sliced
1 large cucumber, cut into large chunks
1 large red pepper, seeded and cut into
    large pieces
1 large yellow pepper, seeded and cut
    into large pieces
1 cup arugula leaves
½ cup chopped fresh basil leaves
½ cup sliced black olives
1 tablespoon capers

Tear bread into large pieces to make about 4 cups. In large bowl, combine olive oil, balsamic vinegar, garlic, salt and TABASCO sauce. Add remaining ingredients; toss to mix well. Let mixture stand 30 minutes before serving.   *Makes 4 servings*

Cream of Pumpkin Curry Soup

3 tablespoons butter
1 cup (1 small) chopped onion
1 clove garlic, finely chopped
1 teaspoon curry powder
½ teaspoon salt
⅛ to ¼ teaspoon ground coriander
⅛ teaspoon crushed red pepper
3 cups water
3 MAGGI® Vegetarian Vegetable
    Bouillon Cubes
1¾ cups (15-ounce can) LIBBY'S® Solid
    Pack Pumpkin
1 cup half-and-half
    Sour cream and chopped fresh chives
    (optional)

Melt butter in large saucepan over medium-high heat. Add onion and garlic; cook for 3 to 5 minutes or until tender. Stir in curry powder, salt, coriander and crushed red pepper; cook for 1 minute. Add water and bouillon; bring to a boil. Reduce heat to low; cook, stirring occasionally, for 15 to 20 minutes. Stir in pumpkin and half-and-half; cook for 5 minutes.

Transfer pumpkin mixture to food processor or blender container (in batches, if necessary); cover. Blend until creamy. Serve warm or reheat to desired temperature. Garnish with dollop of sour cream and chives.   *Makes 4 to 6 servings*

Cool Italian Tomato Soup

Pizzas & Sandwiches

Artichoke Heart, Olive and Goat Cheese Pizza

New York-Style Pizza Crust (recipe
   follows)
2 teaspoons olive oil
2 teaspoons minced fresh rosemary
   leaves *or* 1 teaspoon dried
   rosemary leaves
3 cloves garlic, minced
½ cup (2 ounces) shredded reduced-fat
   Monterey Jack cheese, divided
1 jar (14 ounces) water-packed
   artichoke hearts, drained and
   quartered
3 oil-packed sun-dried tomatoes,
   drained and cut into slices
2½ ounces soft ripe goat cheese, such as
   Montrachet, sliced or crumbled
10 kalamata olives, pitted, halved (about
   ¼ cup)

Prepare New York-Style Pizza Crust. Preheat
oven to 500°F. Brush surface of prepared
crust with olive oil. Sprinkle with rosemary
and garlic; brush again to coat with oil. Bake
on bottom rack of oven about 4 minutes or
until crust begins to turn golden.

Sprinkle with ¼ cup Monterey Jack cheese,
leaving 1-inch border. Top with artichokes,
tomatoes, goat cheese and olives. Sprinkle
with remaining ¼ Monterey Jack cheese.
Return to oven and bake 3 to 4 minutes more
or until crust is deep golden and Monterey
Jack cheese is melted. Cut into 8 wedges.
Makes 4 servings

New York-Style Pizza Crust

⅔ cup warm water (110° to 115°F)
1 teaspoon sugar
½ of ¼-ounce package rapid-rise yeast
   or active dry yeast
1¾ cups all-purpose or bread flour
½ teaspoon salt
1 tablespoon cornmeal (optional)

Combine water and sugar in small bowl; stir
to dissolve sugar. Sprinkle yeast on top; stir
to combine. Let stand 5 minutes until foamy.

Combine flour and salt in large bowl. Stir in
yeast mixture. Mix until mixture forms soft
dough. Remove dough to lightly floured
surface. Knead dough 5 minutes or until
smooth and elastic, adding additional flour
as needed. Place in large bowl coated with
nonstick cooking spray. Turn dough in bowl
so top is coated with cooking spray; cover
with towel or plastic wrap. Let rise in warm
place 30 minutes or until doubled in bulk.

Punch dough down; place on lightly floured
surface and knead 2 minutes or until smooth.
Pat dough into 7-inch disk. Let rest 2 to
3 minutes. Pat and gently stretch dough from
edges until dough seems to not stretch
anymore. Let rest 2 to 3 minutes. Continue
patting and stretching until dough is 12 to
14 inches in diameter. Spray 12- to 14-inch
pizza pan with cooking spray; sprinkle with
cornmeal, if desired. Press dough into pan.
Makes 1 thin 14-inch crust

Artichoke Heart, Olive and Goat Cheese Pizza

Fresh Vegetable Pizza

1 envelope active dry yeast
1 teaspoon sugar
½ cup warm water
3 large cloves CHRISTOPHER
    RANCH Fresh Garlic, divided
1¾ cups sifted all-purpose flour, divided
1 tablespoon oil
1 teaspoon salt, divided
3 small firm ripe tomatoes
1 cup thinly sliced zucchini
1 cup sliced fresh mushrooms
¼ cup sliced green onion
1½ cups (6 ounces) shredded Monterey
    Jack cheese, divided
½ teaspoon dried basil, crushed
½ teaspoon dried Italian herbs
2 tablespoons grated Parmesan cheese

Sprinkle yeast and sugar over warm water; let stand 5 minutes to soften. Peel 1 clove garlic; press through garlic press. Add garlic and ¾ cup flour to yeast; beat until smooth. Stir in oil and ½ teaspoon salt. Gradually stir in remaining 1 cup flour to make moderately stiff dough. Turn out onto floured board and knead about 2 minutes until smooth. Place in greased 10-inch pizza pan and press out to cover pan. Let dough stand while preparing remaining ingredients.

Preheat oven to 375°F. Blanch tomatoes in boiling water to cover. Let stand 10 seconds. Lift out and peel off skins. Remove cores and slice tomatoes about ⅜ inch thick to measure about 2 cups. Blanch zucchini slices in boiling water; cook 1 minute and drain well. Combine with mushrooms and onion. Press remaining 2 cloves garlic; add to vegetables and mix well. Sprinkle 1 cup Monterey Jack cheese over dough. Spoon *half* of vegetable mixture over cheese. Arrange tomato slices on top, overlapping if necessary. Top with remaining vegetable mixture. Sprinkle with herbs, remaining ½ teaspoon salt, ½ cup Monterey Jack cheese and Parmesan cheese. Let stand about 15 minutes until edge of dough feels light to touch. Bake below center of oven about 40 minutes or until edge of crust is nicely browned. Serve warm.

Makes 1 (10-inch) pizza

Eggplant & Pepper Cheese Sandwiches

1 (8-ounce) eggplant, cut into 18 slices
    Salt and pepper, to taste
⅓ cup GREY POUPON® COUNTRY
    DIJON® Mustard
¼ cup olive oil
2 tablespoons REGINA® Red Wine
    Vinegar
¾ teaspoon dried oregano leaves
1 clove garlic, crushed
6 (4-inch) pieces French bread, cut in
    half
1 (7-ounce) jar roasted red peppers, cut
    into strips
1½ cups shredded mozzarella cheese
    (6 ounces)

Place eggplant slices on greased baking sheet, overlapping slightly. Sprinkle lightly with salt and pepper. Bake at 400°F for 10 to 12 minutes or until tender.

Blend mustard, oil, vinegar, oregano and garlic. Brush eggplant slices with ¼ cup mustard mixture; broil eggplant for 1 minute.

Brush cut sides of French bread with remaining mustard mixture. Layer 3 slices eggplant, a few red pepper strips and ¼ cup cheese on each bread bottom. Place on broiler pan with roll tops, cut-sides up; broil until cheese melts. Close sandwiches with bread tops and serve immediately; garnish as desired.

Makes 6 sanwiches

Eggplant & Pepper Cheese Sandwiches

Mexican Deep Dish Pizza

Thick Pizza Crust (recipe follows)
½ small onion, diced
1 teaspoon chili powder
½ teaspoon ground cumin
¼ teaspoon ground cinnamon
1 can (15 ounces) 50%-less-sodium
    black beans, rinsed and drained
½ can (4 ounces) diced green chilies
    (optional)
1 cup (4 ounces) shredded reduced-fat
    Cheddar cheese, divided
¾ cup diced tomatoes
½ cup frozen corn, thawed
½ green bell pepper, diced
½ can (2¼ ounces) sliced black olives,
    drained
½ teaspoon olive oil
    Salsa (optional)
    Reduced-fat sour cream (optional)

Prepare Thick Pizza Crust. Preheat oven to 500°F.

Spray 2- to 3-quart saucepan with cooking spray. Place over medium heat. Add onion, chili powder, cumin, cinnamon and 1 tablespoon water; stir. Cover and cook 3 to 4 minutes. Stir in beans and chilies, if desired. Transfer ½ of bean mixture to food processor; process until almost smooth.

Spread puréed bean mixture over prepared crust up to thick edge. Top with ½ cup cheese, remaining bean mixture, tomatoes, corn, bell pepper and olives. Top with remaining ½ cup cheese. Bake 10 to 12 minutes or until crust is deep golden. Brush crust edge with olive oil. Garnish with cilantro, if desired. Cut into 8 wedges. Serve with salsa and sour cream, if desired.

Makes 4 servings

Thick Pizza Crust

¾ cup warm water (110° to 115°F)
1 teaspoon sugar
½ of ¼-ounce package rapid-rise yeast
    or active dry yeast
2½ cups all-purpose or bread flour
½ teaspoon salt
1 tablespoon cornmeal (optional)

Combine water and sugar in small bowl; stir to dissolve sugar. Sprinkle yeast on top; stir to combine. Let stand 5 minutes until foamy.

Combine flour and salt in large bowl. Stir in yeast mixture. Mix until mixture forms soft dough. Remove dough to lightly floured surface. Knead dough 5 minutes or until smooth and elastic, adding additional flour as needed. Place in bowl coated with nonstick cooking spray. Turn dough in bowl so top is coated with cooking spray; cover with towel or plastic wrap. Let rise in warm place 30 minutes or until doubled in bulk.

Punch dough down; place on lightly floured surface and knead 2 minutes or until smooth. Pat dough into flat disk about 8 to 9 inches in diameter. Let rest 2 to 3 minutes. Pat and gently stretch dough from edges until dough seems to not stretch anymore. Let rest 2 to 3 minutes. Continue patting and stretching until dough is 12 to 14 inches in diameter. Spray 12- to 14-inch pizza pan with nonstick cooking spray; sprinkle with cornmeal, if desired. Press dough into pan. Cover with towel and let stand in warm place 10 to 20 minutes or until slightly puffed.

Preheat oven to 500°F. Prick crust with fork at 2-inch intervals. Bake 4 to 5 minutes or until top is dry but not yet golden. Remove from oven. Follow topping and baking directions for Mexican Deep Dish Pizza, baking pizza on bottom rack of oven.

Makes 1 thick 12-inch crust

Meatless Muffaletta Sandwich

Meatless Muffaletta Sandwich

1 (12-inch) loaf French- or Italian-style
    bread, unsliced
½ cup LAWRY'S® Classic Red Wine
    Vinaigrette with Cabernet
    Sauvignon Dressing
½ cup mayonnaise
2 teaspoons capers
1 ripe avocado, peeled, pitted and sliced
½ cup sliced green Spanish olives
1 can (2¼ ounces) sliced pitted ripe
    olives, drained
4 ounces sliced Swiss cheese
    Fresh basil leaves
4 Roma tomatoes, sliced, or 4 ounces
    roasted red pepper slices
3 thin slices red onion, separated into
    rings

Slice bread horizontally. Hollow out each loaf, leaving ¾-inch shell. (Tear removed bread into crumbs; freeze for another use.) Set bread shells aside. In food processor or blender, place Classic Red Wine Vinaigrette with Cabernet Sauvignon Dressing, mayonnaise and capers; process until well blended. Spread vinaigrette mixture evenly onto insides of shells. Into bottom bread shell, evenly layer remaining ingredients. Cover with top half of bread; press bread halves together firmly. Wrap tightly in plastic wrap; refrigerate 30 minutes.

Makes 4 servings

Presentation: Unwrap loaf; slice into four 3-inch portions. Flavors are best when sandwich is served at room temperature. For crispier crust, place *uncut* loaf in 225°F oven. Bake 15 to 20 minutes. Remove from oven. Cut and fill loaf as directed.

Note: If desired, rinse olives in cold water to reduce saltiness.

Mediterranean Pita Sandwiches

1 cup plain nonfat yogurt
1 tablespoon chopped fresh cilantro
2 garlic cloves, minced
1 teaspoon lemon juice
1½ cups thinly sliced cucumbers, cut into halves
1 can (15 ounces) chick-peas, drained and rinsed
1 can (14 ounces) canned artichoke hearts, drained, rinsed and coarsely chopped
½ cup shredded carrot
½ cup chopped green onions
4 rounds whole wheat pita bread, cut into halves

1. Combine yogurt, cilantro, garlic and lemon juice in a small bowl.

2. Combine cucumbers, chick-peas, artichoke hearts, carrot and green onions in medium bowl. Stir in yogurt mixture until well blended.

3. Divide cucumber mixture among pita halves. Garnish as desired.

Makes 4 servings

California Veggie Rolls

1 package (8 ounces) cream cheese, softened
½ teaspoon LAWRY'S® Garlic Powder with Parsley
½ teaspoon LAWRY'S® Lemon Pepper
6 large or 12 regular-size flour tortillas
1 large bunch fresh spinach leaves, cleaned and stems removed
1½ cups (6 ounces) shredded Cheddar cheese
1½ cups shredded carrots
Fresh salsa

In small bowl, blend together cream cheese, Garlic Powder with Parsley and Lemon Pepper. On each flour tortilla, spread a layer of cream cheese mixture. Layer spinach leaves, Cheddar cheese and carrots over cream cheese mixture. Roll up tortillas. Slice each tortilla into 1½-inch pieces.

Makes 3 dozen

Vegetable Calzone

1 loaf (1 pound) frozen bread dough
1 package (10 ounces) frozen chopped broccoli, thawed and well drained
1 cup (8 ounces) SARGENTO® Light Ricotta Cheese
1 cup (4 ounces) SARGENTO® Classic Shredded Mozzarella Cheese
1 clove garlic, minced
¼ teaspoon white pepper
1 egg beaten with 1 tablespoon water
1 jar (16 ounces) spaghetti sauce, heated (optional)
SARGENTO® Grated Parmesan Cheese (optional)

Thaw bread dough; let rise according to package directions. Combine broccoli, Ricotta and Mozzarella cheeses, garlic and pepper. Punch down bread dough; turn out onto lightly floured surface. Divide into 4 equal pieces. One at a time, roll out each piece into 8-inch circle. Place about ¼ cup cheese mixture on half of circle, leaving 1-inch border. Fold dough over to cover filling, forming semi-circle; press and crimp edges with fork tines to seal. Brush with egg mixture. Place on greased baking sheet; bake at 350°F 30 minutes or until brown and puffed. Transfer to rack; cool 10 minutes. Top with hot spaghetti sauce and Parmesan cheese, if desired. *Makes 4 servings*

Meatless Sloppy Joes

2 cups thinly sliced onions
2 cups chopped green peppers
2 cloves garlic, finely chopped
2 tablespoons ketchup
1 tablespoon mustard
1 can (about 15 ounces) kidney beans, mashed
1 can (8 ounces) tomato sauce
1 teaspoon chili powder
Cider vinegar
2 sandwich rolls, halved

1. Spray large nonstick skillet with cooking spray; heat over medium heat until hot. Add onions, peppers and garlic. Cook and stir 5 minutes or until vegetables are tender. Stir in ketchup and mustard.

2. Add beans, sauce and chili powder. Reduce heat to medium-low. Cook 5 minutes or until thickened, stirring frequently and adding up to $\frac{1}{3}$ cup vinegar if dry. Top sandwich roll halves evenly with bean mixture.   *Makes 4 servings*

Festive Focaccia Pizza Bread

1 pound frozen bread dough, thawed
1½ teaspoons dried Italian herbs
¾ cup (3 ounces) pitted California ripe olives, sliced in thirds (rinse and pat dry before slicing)
¾ cup coarsely chopped California walnuts
1 cup (1 medium) thinly sliced onion
1½ cups (6 ounces) shredded Classic or Hickory Smoked JARLSBERG Cheese
1 tablespoon olive oil
Freshly ground pepper

Pat and stretch dough to fit 12-inch round baking pan. Cover with oiled waxed paper;

Meatless Sloppy Joe

let rise in warm place about 1 hour or until doubled in bulk.

Preheat oven to 375°F. Dimple dough with fingertips, making deep indentations. Sprinkle with herbs, then with olives, walnuts, onion and cheese. Drizzle with oil and sprinkle with pepper to taste.

Bake focaccia in lower third of oven 30 minutes or until golden brown. Serve warm or cool completely, wrap and refrigerate. Reheat before serving.
Makes 10 to 12 servings

Spinach and Tomato Tofu Toss

¾ cup chopped onion
1 teaspoon chopped garlic
1 package (10 ounces) extra-firm tofu, drained and cut into ½-inch cubes
2 teaspoons soy sauce
¼ teaspoon black pepper
¼ pound washed spinach leaves, divided
4 rounds whole wheat pita bread, cut in half
2 large ripe tomatoes, chopped
¾ cup chopped red bell pepper

1. Spray large nonstick skillet with cooking spray; heat over medium heat until hot. Add onion and garlic. Cook and stir 2 minutes or until onion is crisp-tender.

2. Add tofu, soy sauce and black pepper to skillet; toss until well combined. Cook over medium heat 3 to 4 minutes or until heated through. Remove from heat and cool slightly.

3. Set aside 8 whole spinach leaves; tear remaining leaves into bite-size pieces. Line pita halves with whole spinach leaves. Add tomatoes, torn spinach and bell peppers to tofu mixture; toss to combine. Fill pita halves with tofu mixture. Serve immediately.
Makes 4 servings

Enticing Eggs & Cheese

Breakfast Burritos with Tomato-Basil Topping

1 large tomato, diced
2 teaspoons finely chopped basil *or*
  ½ teaspoon dried basil leaves
1 medium potato, peeled and shredded
  (about 1 cup)
¼ cup chopped onion
2 teaspoons FLEISCHMANN'S®
  Margarine
1 cup EGG BEATERS® Healthy Real
  Egg Product
⅛ teaspoon ground black pepper
4 (8-inch) flour tortillas, warmed
⅓ cup shredded reduced-fat Cheddar
  cheese

In small bowl, combine tomato and basil; set aside.

In large nonstick skillet, over medium heat, sauté potato and onion in margarine until tender. Pour Egg Beaters® into skillet; sprinkle with pepper. Cook, stirring occasionally until mixture is set.

Divide egg mixture evenly between tortillas; top with cheese. Fold tortillas over egg mixture. Top with tomato mixture.

Makes 4 servings

Double Onion Quiche

3 cups thinly sliced yellow onions
3 tablespoons butter or margarine
1 cup thinly sliced green onions
3 eggs
1 cup heavy cream
½ cup grated Parmesan cheese
¼ teaspoon hot pepper sauce
1 package (1 ounce) HIDDEN VALLEY
  RANCH® Milk Recipe Original
  Ranch® salad dressing mix
1 (9-inch) deep-dish pastry shell,
  baked, cooled
Fresh oregano sprig for garnish

Preheat oven to 350°F. In medium skillet, cook and stir yellow onions in butter, stirring occasionally, about 10 minutes. Add green onions; cook 5 minutes. Remove from heat; cool.

In large bowl, whisk eggs until frothy. Whisk in cream, cheese, pepper sauce and salad dressing mix. Stir in cooled onion mixture. Pour egg and onion mixture into cooled pastry shell. Bake until top is browned and knife inserted in center comes out clean, 35 to 40 minutes. Cool on wire rack 10 minutes before slicing. Garnish with oregano. *Makes 8 servings*

Breakfast Burritos with Tomato-Basil Topping

31

Asparagus-Swiss Soufflé

¼ cup unsalted butter substitute
½ cup chopped yellow onion
¼ cup all-purpose flour
½ teaspoon salt
¼ teaspoon cayenne pepper
1 cup 2% low-fat milk
1 cup (4 ounces) shredded ALPINE
    LACE® Reduced Fat Swiss Cheese
1 cup egg substitute or 4 large eggs
1 cup coarsely chopped fresh asparagus
    pieces, cooked or frozen asparagus
    pieces, thawed and drained
3 large egg whites

1. Preheat the oven to 325°F. Spray a 1½-quart soufflé dish with nonstick cooking spray.

2. In a large saucepan, melt the butter over medium heat, add the onion and sauté for 5 minutes or until soft. Stir in the flour, salt and pepper and cook for 2 minutes or until bubbly. Add the milk and cook, stirring constantly, for 5 minutes or until the sauce thickens. Add the cheese and stir until melted.

3. In a small bowl, whisk the egg substitute (or the whole eggs). Whisk in a little of the hot cheese sauce, then return the egg mixture to the saucepan and whisk until well blended. Remove from the heat and fold in the drained asparagus.

4. In a medium-size bowl, using an electric mixer set on high, beat the egg whites until stiff peaks form. Fold the hot cheese sauce into the whites, then spoon into the soufflé dish.

5. Place the soufflé on a baking sheet and bake for 50 minutes or until golden brown and puffy. *Makes 8 servings*

Texas Onion Pepper Tart

1 prepared crust for single-layer pie
1 large (14 to 16 ounces) Texas
    SPRINGSWEET® or Texas
    1015 SUPERSWEET® Onion,
    thinly sliced
1 tablespoon butter or margarine
½ cup chopped red bell pepper
¼ cup (2 ounces) diced green chilies
1 cup (4 ounces) shredded hot pepper
    Monterey Jack cheese
1 cup half-and-half
2 eggs
½ teaspoon salt
¼ teaspoon black pepper
¼ teaspoon hot pepper sauce

Press pie crust onto bottom and sides of 9-inch tart pan with removable bottom *or* into 9-inch pie plate; set aside. Sauté onion in butter over medium heat until very soft and golden brown, about 15 minutes. Add bell pepper and green chilies; sauté 2 minutes longer. Refrigerate onion mixture 15 to 20 minutes. Spread onion mixture evenly over bottom of tart crust; top with cheese. Combine half-and-half, eggs, salt, black pepper and pepper sauce in small bowl. Pour over cheese. Bake at 375°F 45 minutes or until filling is golden brown and set.

Makes about 6 servings

Individual Tarts: Cut 8 (4-inch) circles from pie crusts. Press pie crusts onto bottoms and sides of 8 (4-inch) pie tart pans; set aside. Follow directions for single tart, dividing mixtures evenly over each tart crust. Bake at 375°F 30 to 35 minutes or until filling is golden brown and set.

Makes 8 (4-inch) tarts

Asparagus-Swiss Soufflé

Scrambled Eggs Piperade

1 tablespoon vegetable oil
1 medium onion, cut in half and sliced
½ green bell pepper, seeded and sliced
½ red bell pepper, seeded and sliced
4 large eggs
1 tablespoon water
½ teaspoon salt
½ teaspoon TABASCO® pepper sauce
1 tablespoon butter or margarine
  Whole wheat toast

• In 12-inch skillet over medium heat, heat oil until hot. Cook onion and bell peppers until tender-crisp, about 5 minutes, stirring occasionally.

• In medium bowl, beat eggs, water, salt and TABASCO sauce until well blended. In 10-inch nonstick skillet over medium heat, melt butter; add egg mixture. Gently stir egg mixture, lifting it up and over bottom as it thickens. Keep stirring until desired texture and doneness. Serve with pepper mixture and whole wheat toast. *Makes 2 servings*

Asparagus Pie

CRUST
1 cup all-purpose flour
⅛ teaspoon salt
5 tablespoons butter, cut into small
  pieces
3 to 5 tablespoons cold water

FILLING
1 pound asparagus, trimmed
2 tablespoons butter, melted
6 ounces BEL PAESE® semi-soft cheese,
  cut into small pieces
3 eggs
1¼ cups milk
⅛ teaspoon salt

For crust, combine flour and salt. Make well in center. Add butter pieces to well. Mix flour and butter. Add water, 1 tablespoon at a time; mix well. Shape into a ball. Cover and let dough rest for 30 minutes.

Meanwhile, cook asparagus in boiling salted water until tender-crisp, about 5 minutes. Drain and cut into 1-inch pieces. Toss with melted butter.

Preheat oven to 350°F. Grease 9-inch pie plate. Set aside. Roll out dough on floured board. Ease dough into pie plate. Trim and flute edge. Pierce bottom of crust several times with fork. Bake for 5 minutes.

Sprinkle asparagus in bottom of pie crust. Sprinkle cheese over asparagus. In medium mixing bowl, beat eggs, milk and salt. Pour into pie crust. Bake until set and golden brown, 40 to 50 minutes.

Makes 3 main-dish servings

Light Farmhouse Frittata

⅓ cup julienned yellow pepper
⅓ cup julienned green pepper
⅓ cup julienned red pepper
⅓ cup chopped green onions
⅓ cup chopped walnuts
8 egg whites
2 egg yolks
2 tablespoons plain nonfat yogurt
1 tablespoon grated Asiago or
  Parmesan cheese

Preheat oven to 350°F. Cook and stir peppers, green onions and walnuts in ovenproof skillet. Beat egg whites and yolks; add yogurt and pour mixture over vegetables in skillet. Cook and stir over medium heat until eggs begin to set. Sprinkle cheese over top and bake 8 to 10 minutes or until eggs are well set. Cut into wedges to serve.

Makes 4 servings

Favorite recipe from **Walnut Marketing Board**

Cheesey Salsa Omelet

Cheesy Salsa Omelet

1 cup egg substitute
1 tablespoon skim milk
¼ cup sliced fresh mushrooms
¼ cup chopped green onions
¼ cup GUILTLESS GOURMET® Nacho
    Dip (mild or spicy)
¼ cup GUILTLESS GOURMET® Salsa
    (mild, medium or hot)

Combine egg substitute and milk in small bowl; beat well. Coat medium nonstick skillet with nonstick cooking spray; heat over medium-high heat until hot. Add mushrooms and onions; cook and stir 2 to 3 minutes or until vegetables are softened. Remove vegetables from skillet; set aside.

Add egg mixture to same skillet; cook over low heat until egg mixture sets, gently lifting edge with spatula to allow uncooked egg to flow under cooked portion. *Do not stir.* Top with reserved vegetable mixture. Drop spoonfuls nacho dip over vegetable mixture. Cover tightly; let stand 3 to 5 minutes. Fold omelet in half. Gently slide onto warm serving platter. Cut in half; serve each half with 2 tablespoons salsa.

Makes 2 servings

Cheese Blintzes

Basic Crêpes (recipe follows)
1 container (15 ounces) ricotta or light
   ricotta cheese
2 tablespoons powdered sugar
1 teaspoon vanilla
⅛ teaspoon ground nutmeg
1 tablespoon margarine or butter,
   melted
   Additional powdered sugar
   Sour cream
   Applesauce
   Strawberry or raspberry preserves

Prepare Basic Crêpes. Preheat oven to 350°F. Generously grease 13×9-inch baking dish.

Process ricotta cheese, 2 tablespoons powdered sugar, vanilla and nutmeg in food processor about 30 seconds or until smooth. Place about 3 tablespoons cheese mixture in center of each crêpe. Fold bottom edge of crêpe up to partly cover filling; fold in side edges, then roll up completely to enclose filling.

Place blintzes seam side down in prepared dish; brush tops with melted margarine. Bake uncovered 15 to 20 minutes or until heated through. Sprinkle with additional powdered sugar. Serve with sour cream, applesauce and preserves. Garnish as desired. *Makes 4 servings*

Basic Crêpes

1½ cups milk
1 cup all-purpose flour
2 eggs
¼ cup margarine or butter, melted and
   cooled, divided
¼ teaspoon salt

Process milk, flour, eggs, 2 tablespoons margarine and salt in food processor until smooth. Let stand at room temperature 30 minutes.

Heat ½ teaspoon margarine in 7- or 8-inch crêpe pan or skillet over medium heat. Process crêpe batter again until blended. Pour ¼ cup batter into pan. Tilt pan so batter covers bottom of pan. Cook 1 to 2 minutes or until crêpe is brown around edge and top is dry. Carefully turn crêpe with spatula and cook 30 seconds more. Transfer crêpe to waxed paper to cool. Repeat with remaining batter, adding remaining margarine only as needed to prevent sticking.

Separate each crêpe with sheet of waxed paper. Cover and refrigerate up to 1 day or freeze up to 1 month before serving.
Makes about 1 dozen crêpes

Pita in the Morning

1 teaspoon butter or margarine
2 eggs, lightly beaten
¼ teaspoon salt
   Dash pepper
1 whole wheat pita bread, cut in half
¼ cup alfalfa sprouts
2 tablespoons shredded Cheddar cheese
2 tablespoons chopped tomato
   Avocado slices (optional)

1. Melt butter at HIGH 30 seconds in microwavable 1-quart casserole.

2. Season eggs with salt and pepper. Add eggs to casserole. Microwave at HIGH 1½ to 2½ minutes, stirring once. Do not overcook; eggs should be soft with no liquid remaining.

3. Open pita to make pockets. Arrange sprouts in pockets. Divide cheese and eggs evenly between pockets. Top with tomato and avocado slices. *Makes 1 sandwich*

Cheese Blintzes

Triple-Decker Vegetable Omelet

1 cup finely chopped broccoli
½ cup diced red bell pepper
½ cup shredded carrot
⅓ cup sliced green onions
1 clove garlic, minced
2½ teaspoons FLEISCHMANN'S®
    Margarine, divided
¾ cup low-fat cottage cheese
    (1% milkfat), divided
1 tablespoon plain dry bread crumbs
1 tablespoon grated Parmesan cheese
½ teaspoon Italian seasoning
1½ cups EGG BEATERS® Healthy Real
    Egg Product, divided
⅓ cup chopped tomato
    Chopped fresh parsley, for garnish

In 8-inch nonstick skillet, over medium-high heat, sauté broccoli, bell pepper, carrot, green onions and garlic in 1 teaspoon margarine until tender. Remove from skillet; stir in ½ cup cottage cheese. Keep warm. Combine bread crumbs, Parmesan cheese and Italian seasoning; set aside.

In same skillet, over medium heat, melt ½ teaspoon margarine. Pour ½ cup Egg Beaters® into skillet. Cook, lifting edges to allow uncooked portion to flow underneath. When almost set, slide unfolded omelet onto ovenproof serving platter. Top with half each of the vegetable mixture and bread crumb mixture; set aside.

Prepare 2 more omelets with remaining Egg Beaters® and margarine. Layer 1 omelet onto serving platter over vegetable and bread crumb mixture; top with remaining vegetable mixture and bread crumb mixture. Layer with remaining omelet. Top omelet with remaining cottage cheese and tomato. Bake at 425°F for 5 to 7 minutes or until heated through. Garnish with parsley. Cut into wedges to serve. *Makes 4 servings*

Chile Tortilla Brunch Casserole

2 cans (7 ounces each) ORTEGA®
    Whole Green Chiles, split in half,
    divided
6 corn tortillas, cut into strips, divided
4 cups (16 ounces) shredded Monterey
    Jack cheese, divided
1 cup (1 medium) chopped tomato
4 tablespoons (3) chopped green
    onions, divided
8 eggs
½ cup milk
½ teaspoon salt
½ teaspoon ground black pepper
½ teaspoon ground cumin
    ORTEGA® Thick & Chunky Salsa,
    hot, medium or mild

LAYER *1 can* of chiles, *3* tortillas and *2 cups* cheese in greased 9-inch-square baking pan. Top with tomato and *2 tablespoons* green onions; layer *remaining 1 can* chiles, *remaining 3* tortillas and *remaining 2 cups* cheese over tomato. Beat eggs, milk, salt, pepper and cumin in medium bowl; pour over chile mixture.

BAKE in preheated 350°F. oven for 40 to 45 minutes or until center is set. Cool for 10 minutes; sprinkle with *remaining 2 tablespoons* green onions. Serve with salsa. *Makes 8 servings*

Triple-Decker Vegetable Omelet

Grains & Beans

Roasted Corn & Wild Rice Salad

½ cup uncooked wild rice
1½ cups fresh corn (about 3 medium ears)
½ cup diced seeded tomato
½ cup finely chopped yellow or green bell pepper
⅓ cup minced fresh cilantro
2 tablespoons minced seeded jalapeño peppers* (optional)
2 tablespoons fresh lime juice
2 tablespoons prepared honey mustard
1 tablespoon olive oil
½ teaspoon ground cumin

Jalapeño peppers can sting and irritate the skin; wear rubber gloves when handling peppers and do not touch eyes.

1. Place 1½ cups water in small saucepan; bring to a boil over high heat. Stir in wild rice; cover. Reduce heat to medium-low. Simmer 40 minutes or until rice is just tender but still firm to the bite. Drain rice; discard liquid.

2. Preheat oven to 400°F. Spray baking sheet with nonstick cooking spray.

3. Spread corn evenly over prepared baking sheet. Bake 20 to 25 minutes or until corn is lightly browned, stirring after 15 minutes.

4. Combine rice, corn, tomato, bell pepper, cilantro and jalapeños in large bowl. Combine lime juice, honey mustard, oil and cumin in small bowl until well blended. Drizzle over rice mixture; toss to coat. Cover; refrigerate 2 hours. Serve on lettuce leaves, if desired. *Makes 6 servings*

Tex-Mex Barley Bake

1 small onion, chopped
1 small green bell pepper, diced
1 tablespoon vegetable oil
1 clove garlic, chopped
3 cups cooked pinto beans
2 cups medium pearled barley, cooked
1 can (15 ounces) Mexican-style stewed tomatoes, drained, chopped
1 cup sliced pitted ripe olives
1½ teaspoons chili powder
½ teaspoon salt
½ teaspoon ground cumin
1 cup (4 ounces) shredded Cheddar cheese

Cook and stir onion and green bell pepper in oil over medium-low heat 10 minutes. Add garlic. Cook and stir 1 minute. Add remaining ingredients except cheese. Pour into 6 lightly greased individual casseroles. Bake in preheated 350°F oven 35 to 40 minutes or until hot and bubbly. Stir in cheese. Bake 10 minutes or until cheese is melted. *Makes 6 servings*

Favorite recipe from **North Dakota Barley Council**

Roasted Corn & Wild Rice Salad

Vegetable Risotto

2 tablespoons olive oil, divided
1 medium zucchini, cubed
1 medium yellow squash, cubed
1 cup shiitake mushroom slices
1 cup chopped onions
1 clove garlic, minced
6 plum tomatoes, stemmed, seeded and
  quartered
1 teaspoon dried oregano leaves
3 cups Vegetable Stock (page 16)
¾ cup arborio rice
¼ cup grated Parmesan cheese
  Salt
  Black pepper
½ cup frozen peas, thawed
  Fresh oregano for garnish

Heat 1 tablespoon oil in large saucepan over medium heat until hot. Add zucchini and squash; cook and stir 5 minutes or until crisp-tender. Place in medium bowl; set aside. Add mushrooms, onions and garlic to saucepan; cook and stir 5 minutes or until tender. Add tomatoes and oregano; cook and stir 2 to 3 minutes or until tomatoes are soft. Place in bowl with zucchini mixture. Wipe saucepan clean with paper towels.

Place stock in small saucepan; bring to a boil over medium heat. Reduce heat to medium-low to keep stock hot, but not boiling.

Meanwhile, heat remaining 1 tablespoon oil in saucepan over medium heat until hot. Add rice; cook and stir 2 minutes. Add ¾ cup stock to rice. Reduce heat to medium-low, maintaining a simmer. Cook and stir until rice has absorbed stock. Repeat, adding stock 3 more times, cooking and stirring until rice has absorbed stock, about 20 to 25 minutes.

Stir cheese into rice mixture. Season to taste with salt and pepper. Stir in reserved vegetables and peas; cook until heated through. Serve immediately. Garnish, if desired. *Makes 4 to 6 servings*

Eggplant Bulgur Casserole

1 cup bulgur wheat
½ cup chopped green pepper
¼ cup chopped onion
¼ cup butter
4 cups cubed peeled eggplant
1 (15-ounce) can tomato sauce
1 (14½-ounce) can tomatoes,
  undrained, cut up
½ cup cold water
½ teaspoon dried oregano leaves,
  crushed
1 (8-ounce) package PHILADELPHIA
  BRAND® Cream Cheese, softened
1 egg
  KRAFT® 100% Grated Parmesan
  Cheese

• Preheat oven to 350°F.

• Sauté bulgur wheat, peppers and onions in butter in large skillet until vegetables are tender.

• Stir in eggplant, tomato sauce, tomatoes, water and oregano. Cover; simmer 15 to 20 minutes or until eggplant is tender, stirring occasionally.

• Beat cream cheese and egg in small mixing bowl at medium speed with electric mixer until well blended.

• Place half of vegetable mixture in 1½-quart baking dish or casserole; top with cream cheese mixture and remaining vegetable mixture. Cover.

• Bake 15 minutes. Remove cover; sprinkle with Parmesan cheese. Continue baking 10 minutes or until thoroughly heated.
Makes 8 to 10 servings

Vegetable Risotto

Black Bean-and-Barley Salad

¾ **cup barley, uncooked**
¼ **cup lime juice**
 2 **tablespoons water**
 1 **tablespoon vegetable oil**
 1 **teaspoon sugar**
½ **teaspoon garlic powder**
¼ **teaspoon salt**
¼ **teaspoon ground black pepper**
¼ **teaspoon ground cumin**
¼ **teaspoon ground red pepper**
 1 **(15-ounce) can black beans, rinsed**
    and drained
   Leaf lettuce
 1 **cup chopped tomato**
¼ **cup (1 ounce) HEALTHY CHOICE®**
    Fat Free Cheddar Shreds
¼ **cup sliced green onions**

Cook barley according to package directions, omitting salt and fat. Drain and set aside.

Combine lime juice and next 8 ingredients in jar. Cover tightly and shake vigorously.

Pour half of lime juice mixture over barley; cover and refrigerate at least 8 hours, stirring occasionally.

Combine black beans and remaining lime juice mixture; cover and refrigerate at least 8 hours, stirring occasionally.

Spoon barley mixture evenly onto lettuce-lined plates. Top evenly with black beans, tomato, cheese, and green onions.

Makes 4 to 6 servings

Black Bean-and-Barley Salad

Mediterranean Couscous

1 (10-ounce) package couscous
⅓ cup GREY POUPON® COUNTRY DIJON® Mustard
¼ cup lemon juice
¼ cup chopped parsley
3 tablespoons chopped fresh mint
1 tablespoon grated lemon peel
1 clove garlic, minced
⅔ cup olive oil
1 (7-ounce) jar roasted red peppers, drained and chopped
4 ounces feta cheese, diced
½ cup chopped pitted ripe olives
   Sliced tomatoes and cucumbers, for garnish

Prepare couscous according to package directions; cool.

In small bowl, whisk mustard, lemon juice, parsley, mint, lemon peel and garlic until blended. Whisk in oil.

In large bowl, combine couscous, peppers, cheese and olives; add mustard mixture, tossing to coat well. Chill at least 1 hour. To serve, arrange couscous mixture on serving plate; garnish with tomato and cucumber slices. *Makes 6 servings*

Pearls o' Barley Salad

2 cups water
½ cup QUAKER® Scotch Brand Pearled Barley*
⅛ teaspoon salt (optional)
½ cup (2 ounces) cubed Swiss cheese
½ medium cucumber, cut into match stick pieces
⅓ cup sliced celery
⅓ cup sliced green onions
¼ cup finely chopped fresh parsley
¼ cup sliced green olives
¼ cup Italian salad dressing
¼ teaspoon dried oregano leaves, crumbled
⅛ to ¼ teaspoon ground red pepper
   Fresh spinach leaves, rinsed, trimmed
2 to 3 tablespoons dry roasted sunflower kernels

Quick Method: Use ⅔ cup QUAKER® Scotch Brand Quick Pearled Barley; decrease simmer time to 10 to 12 minutes. Proceed as directed.

Bring water to a boil; stir in barley and salt. Cover and reduce heat. Simmer 45 to 50 minutes or until tender. Remove from heat; let stand 5 minutes.

In large bowl, combine barley with remaining ingredients except spinach leaves and sunflower kernels. Marinate several hours or overnight. Serve on large platter or individual plates lined with spinach leaves. Sprinkle with sunflower kernels. Garnish with tomato wedges, if desired.

Makes 8 servings

Bean Salad with Bulgur

¾ cup uncooked dried red kidney beans,
  sorted and rinsed
¾ cup uncooked dried pinto beans,
  sorted and rinsed
8 ounces fresh green beans, cut into
  2-inch pieces
½ cup uncooked bulgur
1 cup water
⅓ cup vegetable oil
1 tablespoon Oriental sesame oil
6 green onions with tops, chopped
2 tablespoons minced fresh ginger
3 cloves garlic, minced
¼ teaspoon crushed red pepper
3 tablespoons soy sauce
2 tablespoons white wine vinegar
½ teaspoon sugar

Soak kidney and pinto beans overnight in cold water; rinse and drain. Place in large saucepan and cover with 6 cups water. Bring to a boil; reduce heat to low. Cover and simmer 1 hour or until tender. Rinse; drain and set aside. Meanwhile, place green beans in 2-quart saucepan; cover with water. Bring to a boil over medium-high heat. Reduce heat to low; simmer, covered, 5 to 6 minutes until beans are crisp-tender. Rinse; drain and set aside.

Combine bulgur and 1 cup water in 1-quart saucepan. Bring to a boil over medium heat. Reduce heat to low; simmer, covered, 15 minutes or until water is absorbed and bulgur is fluffy.

Combine green beans, bulgur, kidney and pinto beans in large bowl.

Heat vegetable oil and sesame oil in large skillet over medium heat. Add onions, ginger, garlic and crushed red pepper. Cook and stir about 3 minutes or until onions are tender. Remove from heat. Stir in soy sauce, vinegar and sugar. Pour oil mixture into bean mixture; mix well. Cover; refrigerate 2 to 3 hours. Garnish, if desired.

Makes 6 to 8 servings

Mexicali Wild Rice Casserole

2 cups cooked wild rice
1 can (about 17 ounces) whole kernel
  corn, drained
1 can (about 4 ounces) chopped or
  diced green chilies, drained
2 cups (16 ounces) chunky, mild salsa
  (use medium for hotter flavor)
1 cup grated Cheddar or Monterey
  Jack cheese
Corn or tortilla chips

Combine wild rice with corn and chilies and spread in lightly oiled 11×7-inch casserole. Spread salsa over mixture and sprinkle with cheese. Cover and heat at 350°F about 30 minutes. Serve with a basket of corn or tortilla chips. *Makes 4 servings*

Serving Suggestion: To serve individual servings, heat casserole ingredients without cheese and spoon over corn or tortilla chips on individual plates; sprinkle cheese on top and, if desired, heat either under a broiler or in a microwave to melt cheese.

Favorite recipe from **Minnesota Cultivated Wild Rice Council**

Bean Salad with Bulgur

Tabbouleh

¾ cup bulgur, rinsed, drained
  Boiling water
2 cups chopped seeded cucumber
1 large tomato, seeded, chopped
1 cup snipped parsley
⅓ cup chopped green onions
⅓ cup CRISCO® Oil or CRISCO®
  PURITAN® Canola Oil
2 tablespoons lemon juice
1 teaspoon dried mint leaves, crumbled
2 cloves garlic, minced
½ teaspoon salt
⅛ teaspoon white pepper
⅛ teaspoon ground red pepper

Place bulgur in medium mixing bowl. Add enough boiling water to just cover bulgur. Let stand about 1 hour or until bulgur is rehydrated. Drain.

Combine bulgur, cucumber, tomato and parsley in large serving bowl; set aside. Blend remaining ingredients in small mixing bowl. Pour over bulgur mixture; toss to coat. Cover; refrigerate at least 3 hours. Stir before serving.   *Makes 10 to 12 servings*

Encore Salad

1½ cups white vinegar
1 cup olive oil
¼ cup sugar
2 teaspoons salt
¾ teaspoon black pepper
1 clove garlic, minced
12 pearl onions or very small onions
1 cup water
1 small cauliflower, cut into florets
2 cups canned black-eyed peas, rinsed
  and drained
1 (15-ounce) can beets, drained, cut
  into quarters
1 green pepper, cut into ½-inch strips
1 (6-ounce) can ripe olives, drained,
  halved

Combine vinegar, oil, sugar, salt, pepper and garlic in medium saucepan. Bring to a boil over high heat, stirring constantly; cool 5 minutes. Add onions and water; bring to a boil. Cover and reduce heat; simmer 2 minutes or until onions are tender. Drain. Add cauliflower, black-eyed peas, beets, green pepper and olives; refrigerate 8 hours, stirring occasionally.   *Makes 6 servings*

Favorite recipe from **Black-Eyed Pea Jamboree—Athens, Texas**

Brown Rice Black Bean Burrito

1 tablespoon vegetable oil
1 medium onion, chopped
2 cloves garlic, minced
1½ teaspoons chili powder
½ teaspoon ground cumin
3 cups cooked brown rice
1 (15- to 16-ounce) can black beans,
  drained and rinsed
1 (11-ounce) can corn, drained
6 (8-inch) flour tortillas
¾ cup (6 ounces) shredded reduced-fat
  Cheddar cheese
2 green onions, thinly sliced
¼ cup plain low-fat yogurt
¼ cup prepared salsa

Heat oil in large skillet over medium-high heat until hot. Add onion, garlic, chili powder and cumin. Sauté 3 to 5 minutes until onion is tender. Add rice, beans and corn; cook, stirring 2 to 3 minutes until mixture is thoroughly heated. Remove from heat.

Spoon ½ cup rice mixture down center of each tortilla. Top each evenly with cheese, green onions and yogurt. Roll up and top evenly with salsa.   *Makes 6 servings*

Favorite recipe from **USA Rice Council**

Tabbouleh

Glorious Garbanzo Salad

5 cups cooked low-sodium garbanzo beans, well drained
3 medium-sized tomatoes, diced
⅓ cup chopped toasted* California Walnuts
¼ cup chopped parsley
¼ cup chopped green onions
½ cup nonfat cottage cheese
3 tablespoons wine vinegar
1 tablespoon olive oil
1 clove garlic, minced
1 teaspoon salt
½ teaspoon freshly ground pepper

*Toasting walnuts is optional.

Rinse beans under running water, then drain well again. Place in medium bowl. Add tomatoes, walnuts, parsley and green onions; set aside.

In small bowl, whisk together cottage cheese, vinegar, oil, garlic, salt and pepper. Pour over salad ingredients and toss to combine. Chill before serving, tossing occasionally. Taste and season with additional pepper and vinegar, if necessary.

Makes 8 servings

Favorite recipe from **Walnut Marketing Board**

Brown Rice Primavera

1¼ cups water
½ cup long-grain brown rice, uncooked
½ teaspoon salt
¼ teaspoon dried basil leaves, crumbled
⅛ teaspoon black pepper
1 tablespoon CRISCO® Oil
1 carrot, peeled, diced (about ½ cup)
1 small zucchini, diced (about ½ cup)
1 small yellow squash, diced (about ½ cup)
1 small red bell pepper, seeded, diced (about ½ cup)
2 green onions, thinly sliced

1. Bring water to a boil in medium saucepan on medium heat. Add rice, salt, basil and black pepper. Reduce heat to low. Cover; simmer 40 to 45 minutes or until water is absorbed and rice is tender.

2. Heat Crisco® Oil in large skillet on medium-high heat. Add carrot, zucchini, yellow squash, red pepper and green onions. Cook and stir 5 to 7 minutes or until tender.

3. Transfer rice to serving bowl. Add vegetables; toss to combine. Serve immediately. *Makes 4 servings*

Three-Pepper Risotto

2 tablespoons olive or vegetable oil
3 medium red, green and/or yellow bell peppers, diced
1½ cups arborio, regular or converted rice
½ cup dry white wine, vermouth or water
1 envelope LIPTON® Recipe Secrets® Savory Herb with Garlic Soup Mix*
3½ cups boiling water
½ cup grated Parmesan cheese

In heavy-duty 3-quart saucepan, heat oil over medium-high heat and cook bell peppers, stirring occasionally, 5 minutes. Add rice and cook, stirring constantly, 3 minutes. Slowly add wine and cook, stirring constantly, until liquid is absorbed. Stir in savory herb with garlic soup mix blended with 1 cup boiling water. Reduce heat to low and simmer uncovered, stirring frequently, until liquid is absorbed. Continue adding remaining 2½ cups boiling water, 1 cup at a time, stirring frequently, until rice is slightly creamy and just tender. Stir in cheese. *Makes about 4 servings*

Note: Also terrific with Lipton® Recipe Secrets® Golden Herb with Lemon, Onion, Golden Onion or Onion-Mushroom Soup Mix.

French Lentil Salad

French Lentil Salad

¼ cup chopped walnuts
1½ cups dried lentils, rinsed, sorted and
    drained
4 green onions, finely chopped
3 tablespoons balsamic vinegar
2 tablespoons chopped fresh parsley
1 tablespoon olive oil
¾ teaspoon salt
½ teaspoon dried thyme leaves
¼ teaspoon ground black pepper

1. Preheat oven to 375°F.

2. Spread walnuts in even layer over baking sheet. Bake 5 minutes or until lightly browned. Remove from oven. Cool completely on baking sheet.

3. Combine 2 quarts water and lentils in large saucepan; bring to a boil over high heat. Cover; reduce heat to medium-low. Simmer 30 minutes or until lentils are tender, stirring occasionally. Drain lentils; discard liquid.

4. Combine lentils, onions, vinegar, parsley, oil, salt, thyme and pepper in large bowl. Cover; refrigerate 1 hour or until cool.

5. Serve on lettuce leaves, if desired. Top with walnuts before serving. Garnish as desired. *Makes 4 servings*

Louisiana Red Beans & Rice

1 package (7.2 ounces) **RICE-A-RONI®**
   Herb & Butter
1 cup chopped green or yellow bell
   pepper
¾ cup chopped onion
2 cloves garlic, minced
2 tablespoons vegetable oil or olive oil
1 can (15 or 16 ounces) red beans or
   kidney beans, rinsed and drained
1 can (14½ or 16 ounces) tomatoes or
   stewed tomatoes, undrained
1 teaspoon dried thyme leaves or dried
   oregano leaves
⅛ teaspoon hot pepper sauce or black
   pepper
2 tablespoons chopped parsley
   (optional)

1. Prepare Rice-A-Roni® Mix as package
directs.

2. While Rice-A-Roni® is simmering, in
second large skillet, sauté green pepper,
onion and garlic in oil 5 minutes.

3. Stir in beans, tomatoes, thyme and hot
pepper sauce. Simmer, uncovered,
10 minutes, stirring occasionally. Stir in
parsley. Serve over rice.

Makes 5 servings

Lentils, Olives and Feta

3 cups vegetable broth
1¾ cups (12 ounces) lentils, rinsed and
   drained
1 clove garlic, minced
½ teaspoon dried basil
   Mint Dressing (recipe follows)
4 cups spinach leaves, rinsed and
   crisped
1 cup California Ripe Olives, sliced
⅓ cup thinly sliced green onions
½ cup crumbled feta cheese
   Mint sprigs (optional)

Bring broth to boil. Stir in lentils, garlic and
basil. Reduce heat, cover and simmer until
lentils are tender to bite, about 30 minutes.
While lentils are cooking, prepare Mint
Dressing and set aside. Finely shred 2 cups
spinach leaves; cover and set aside. Remove
pan from heat and drain lentils, if necessary.
Gently stir in olives, shredded spinach and
onions. Spoon lentil mixture over remaining
spinach leaves on platter and sprinkle with
cheese. Drizzle with Mint Dressing and
garnish with mint sprigs, if desired.
Makes about 8 cups; 6 to 8 servings

Mint Dressing: Beat to blend ⅓ cup lemon
juice, 3 tablespoons olive oil, 2 teaspoons
honey, and ⅛ teaspoon *each* salt and pepper.
Just before serving, stir in 3 tablespoons
chopped fresh mint.

Favorite recipe from **California Olive Industry**

Louisiana Red Beans & Rice

Curried Vegetables

1 package (7.2 ounces) RICE-A-RONI®
    Herb & Butter
⅓ cup raisins
2 tablespoons margarine or butter
1 medium onion, chopped
2 cloves garlic, minced
1 tablespoon all-purpose flour
2 teaspoons curry powder
1 package (16 ounces) frozen mixed
    carrot, broccoli and red pepper
    vegetable medley
1 cup water
½ teaspoon salt (optional)
¼ cup slivered almonds, toasted
    (optional)

1. Prepare Rice-A-Roni® Mix as package directs, adding raisins with contents of seasoning packet.

2. In 3-quart saucepan, melt margarine over medium heat. Add onion and garlic; sauté 3 to 4 minutes. Add flour and curry powder; cook 30 seconds, stirring frequently.

3. Add frozen vegetables, water and salt. Cover; bring to a boil over high heat. Cover; reduce heat. Continue cooking 10 minutes, stirring occasionally.

4. Serve rice topped with vegetable mixture; sprinkle with almonds.

Makes 4 servings

Apricot Couscous Pilaf

½ tablespoon butter
½ tablespoon vegetable oil
½ cup thinly sliced green onions
½ cup finely diced red bell pepper
½ teaspoon ground cumin
1 (16-ounce) can apricot halves,
    drained and diced
¼ teaspoon salt
¼ teaspoon ground black pepper
3½ cups cooked instant couscous or
    white or brown rice
2 tablespoons chopped fresh coriander
    (cilantro) or parsley

Melt butter with oil over medium-high heat in large saucepan. Stir in onions, bell pepper and cumin. Sauté 5 minutes or until vegetables are tender. Add diced apricot, salt and pepper; cook 1 minute. Stir in cooked couscous or rice until all ingredients are well combined; cook, stirring constantly. Remove from heat; stir in coriander or parsley.

Serve as stuffing for bell peppers. Also, perfect as light entrée with tossed salad and bread.
    Makes 8 servings

Favorite recipe from **California Apricot Advisory Board**

Apricot Couscous Pilaf

Family-Pleasing Pastas

Pasta with Onions and Goat Cheese

2 teaspoons olive oil
4 cups thinly sliced sweet onions
¾ cup (3 ounces) goat cheese
¼ cup skim milk
6 ounces uncooked baby bow tie or other small pasta
1 clove garlic, minced
2 tablespoons dry white wine
1½ teaspoons chopped fresh sage or ½ teaspoon dried sage leaves
½ teaspoon salt
¼ teaspoon pepper
2 tablespoons chopped toasted walnuts

Heat oil in large nonstick skillet over medium heat. Add onions; cook slowly until golden and caramelized, about 20 to 25 minutes, stirring occasionally.

Combine goat cheese and milk in small bowl; stir until well blended. Set aside.

Cook pasta according to package directions, omitting salt. Drain and set aside.

Add garlic to onions in skillet; cook until softened, about 3 minutes. Add wine, sage, salt and pepper; cook until moisture is evaporated. Remove from heat; add pasta and goat cheese mixture, stirring to melt cheese. Sprinkle with walnuts.

Makes 4 servings

Hearty Manicotti

1 package (10 ounces) frozen chopped spinach, thawed, squeezed dry
2 cups (15-ounce container) ricotta cheese
1 egg, lightly beaten
½ cup (2 ounces) grated Parmesan cheese
⅛ teaspoon ground black pepper
8 to 10 dry manicotti shells, cooked, drained
1⅓ cups (two 6-ounce cans) CONTADINA® Italian Paste
1⅓ cups water
½ cup (2 ounces) shredded mozzarella cheese

In medium bowl, combine spinach, ricotta cheese, egg, Parmesan cheese and pepper; mix well. Spoon into manicotti shells. Place in ungreased 12×7½-inch baking dish. In small bowl, combine tomato paste and water; pour over manicotti. Sprinkle with mozzarella cheese. Bake in preheated 350°F. oven for 30 to 40 minutes or until heated through.

Makes 4 to 5 servings

Hearty Manicotti

Pasta with Spinach-Cheese Sauce

¼ cup FILIPPO BERIO® Extra-Virgin Flavorful Olive Oil, divided
1 medium onion, chopped
1 clove garlic, chopped
3 cups chopped fresh spinach, washed and well drained
1 cup low-fat ricotta or cottage cheese
½ cup chopped fresh parsley
1 teaspoon dried basil leaves, crushed
1 teaspoon lemon juice
¼ teaspoon black pepper
¼ teaspoon ground nutmeg
¾ pound uncooked spaghetti

1. Heat 3 tablespoons olive oil in large skillet over medium heat. Add onion and garlic; cook and stir until onion is tender.

2. Add spinach to skillet; cook 3 to 5 minutes or until spinach wilts.

3. Place spinach mixture, cheese, parsley, basil, lemon juice, pepper and nutmeg in covered blender container. Blend until smooth. Leave in blender, covered, to keep sauce warm.

4. Cook pasta according to package directions until tender. Do not overcook. Drain pasta, reserving ¼ cup water. Toss pasta with remaining 1 tablespoon olive oil in large bowl.

5. Add reserved ¼ cup water to sauce in blender. Blend; serve sauce over pasta.

Makes 4 servings

Italian Garden Fusilli

1¾ cups (14.5-ounce can) CONTADINA® Recipe Ready Diced Tomatoes, undrained
1 cup (4 ounces) cut fresh green beans
½ teaspoon garlic salt
¼ teaspoon dried rosemary leaves, crushed
1 small zucchini, thinly sliced (about 1 cup)
1 small yellow squash, thinly sliced (about 1 cup)
1 cup (12-ounce jar) marinated artichoke hearts, undrained
1 cup frozen peas
½ teaspoon salt, or to taste
¼ teaspoon ground black pepper, or to taste
8 ounces dry fusilli, cooked, drained, kept warm
¼ cup (1 ounce) shredded Parmesan cheese

In large skillet, combine tomatoes and juice, green beans, garlic salt and rosemary. Bring to a boil. Reduce heat to low; cover. Simmer for 3 minutes. Add zucchini and yellow squash; cover. Simmer for 3 minutes or until vegetables are tender. Stir in artichoke hearts and juice, peas, salt and pepper; heat through. Add pasta; toss to coat well. Sprinkle with Parmesan cheese just before serving. *Makes 6 to 8 servings*

Italian Garden Fusilli

FAMILY–PLEASING PASTAS 59

Linguine with Sun-Dried Tomato Pesto

½ cup sun-dried tomatoes
½ cup loosely packed fresh basil
1 teaspoon dried oregano leaves
1 clove garlic, minced
2 tablespoons olive oil
1½ tablespoons grated Parmesan cheese
8 ounces linguine or angel hair pasta,
   cooked and kept warm

1. Combine sun-dried tomatoes with ½ cup hot water in small bowl; soak 3 to 5 minutes or until tomatoes are soft and pliable. Drain; reserve liquid.

2. Combine tomatoes, basil, oregano, garlic, oil and cheese in food processor or blender. Process, adding enough reserved liquid 1 teaspoon at a time, until mixture is of medium to thick sauce consistency. Spoon over pasta and toss; serve immediately.

Makes 4 servings

Porcini Mushroom Penne Rigate with Garlic Butter Sauce

1 (12-ounce) package PASTA
   LABELLA® Porcini Mushroom
   Penne Rigate
2 tablespoons butter
1 tablespoon extra virgin olive oil
1½ cups chopped mushrooms
2 teaspoons minced garlic
¾ cup white wine
¼ cup minced green onions
2 tablespoons lemon juice
¼ cup grated Parmesan cheese
1½ tablespoons chopped parsley

Cook pasta according to package directions. Heat butter and olive oil in large skillet; sauté mushrooms and garlic over medium heat for 4 minutes. Add wine, green onions and lemon juice to skillet and simmer. Mix in hot porcini mushroom penne rigate; sprinkle with cheese and parsley and serve.

Makes 3 servings

Pennini with Vegetable Sauce "Springtime"

12 ounces (3 cups) uncooked mostaccioli
1 red bell pepper
2 small zucchini
⅔ cup fresh Oriental pea pods or
   10 ounces frozen pea pods
3 green onions
4 tablespoons olive oil
2 carrots, cut into julienne strips
1½ cups diced fresh tomatoes
2 tablespoons chopped chives
2 tablespoons fresh chopped dill *or*
   ½ teaspoon dried dill weed
Salt and fresh ground pepper
¼ cup toasted sunflower kernels

Cook pasta according to package directions; drain well. Cut red pepper and zucchini into small slices. Cut pea pods in half or thirds and slice green onions. While pasta is cooking, heat oil in large nonstick saucepan over medium heat. Add red pepper and carrots; cook and stir 6 minutes. Add zucchini, pea pods and onions; cook and stir an additional 5 minutes. Add tomatoes, chives and dill. Season with salt and pepper. Heat until warmed through. Toss vegetable mixture with cooked pasta. Sprinkle with toasted sunflower kernels. Serve hot.

Makes 4 servings

Favorite recipe from **National Sunflower Association**

Linguine with Sun-Dried Tomato Pesto

Penne with Tomatoes, Basil Leaves and Blue Cheese

Penne with Tomatoes, Basil Leaves and Blue Cheese

12 ripe plum tomatoes (about 1½ pounds), quartered or 1 pint cherry tomatoes, cut into halves

2 cups lightly packed whole fresh basil leaves

½ cup (2 ounces) finely crumbled blue cheese

2 tablespoons olive or vegetable oil

2 tablespoons white wine vinegar Salt and pepper to taste

1 pound Penne, Mostaccioli, or other medium pasta shape, uncooked

Toss tomatoes, basil, cheese, oil and vinegar in large bowl. Season to taste with salt and pepper. Refrigerate and let marinate 45 minutes to 24 hours.

Cook pasta according to package directions. When pasta is done, drain well. Add pasta to tomato mixture and toss to mix. Let stand at room temperature about 15 minutes before serving. *Makes 12 servings*

Note: Use smallest basil leaves for recipe. If leaves are longer than an inch long, tear in half crosswise before adding to tomato mixture.

Favorite recipe from **National Pasta Association**

Broccoli and Cauliflower Linguine

2 tablespoons olive or vegetable oil
2 cups broccoli florets
2 cups cauliflower florets
3 cloves garlic, minced
3½ cups (28-ounce can) CONTADINA®
    Pasta Ready Chunky Tomatoes
    with Olive Oil, Garlic, Basil and
    Spices, undrained
1 teaspoon salt
¼ teaspoon crushed red pepper flakes
½ cup dry sherry or chicken broth
1 pound dry linguine, cooked, drained,
    kept warm
½ cup (2 ounces) grated Romano cheese
½ cup finely chopped fresh cilantro

In large skillet, heat oil. Add broccoli, cauliflower and garlic; sauté for 3 minutes. Add tomatoes and juice, salt and red pepper flakes. Bring to a boil. Reduce heat to low; simmer, uncovered, for 20 minutes, stirring occasionally. Add sherry; simmer for 3 minutes. In large bowl, place pasta. Add vegetable mixture, cheese and cilantro; toss to coat well. *Makes 8 servings*

Vegetable Lo Mein

8 ounces uncooked vermicelli or thin
    spaghetti, cooked and drained
¾ teaspoon Oriental sesame oil
½ teaspoon vegetable oil
3 cloves garlic, minced
1 teaspoon grated fresh ginger
2 cups sliced bok choy
½ cup sliced green onions
2 cups shredded carrots
6 ounces firm tofu, drained and cubed
6 tablespoons rice wine vinegar
¼ cup plum preserves
¼ cup water
1 teaspoon reduced-sodium soy sauce
½ teaspoon crushed red pepper flakes

Toss vermicelli with sesame oil in large bowl until well coated. Heat vegetable oil in large nonstick skillet or wok over medium heat. Stir in garlic and ginger; stir-fry 10 seconds. Add bok choy and onions; stir-fry 3 to 4 minutes until crisp-tender. Add carrots and tofu; stir-fry 2 to 3 minutes until carrots are crisp-tender.

Combine vinegar, preserves, water, soy sauce and crushed red pepper in small saucepan. Heat over medium heat until preserves are melted, stirring constantly. Combine noodles, vegetable mixture and sauce in large bowl; mix well.
Makes 6 servings

Cheese Ravioli with Wild Mushroom Sauce

2 tablespoons olive oil
1 medium onion, chopped
1 clove garlic, minced
8 ounces firm tofu
1½ cups ricotta cheese
1 cup grated Parmesan cheese, divided
½ teaspoon dried rosemary leaves
¼ teaspoon salt
64 plain or colored wonton wrappers
    (about 1⅓ packages)
    Wild Mushroom Sauce (recipe
    follows)

Heat oil in small skillet over medium heat until hot. Add onion and garlic; cook and stir 5 minutes or until tender. Place in medium bowl.

Drain tofu on paper towels. Cut into 1-inch cubes. Process tofu, ricotta cheese, ⅓ cup Parmesan cheese, rosemary and salt in food processor until smooth. Stir into onion mixture in bowl.

To make ravioli, work with 8 wonton wrappers at a time, keeping remaining wrappers covered with plastic wrap. Place about 1 tablespoon cheese mixture in center of each wrapper. Brush edges of wrappers with water. Place second wrapper over filling and press edges together to seal. Cover with plastic wrap and set aside. Repeat with remaining wrappers and cheese mixture. Prepare Wild Mushroom Sauce; keep warm.

Bring 3 quarts water to a boil in Dutch oven over high heat. Place 8 ravioli in water. Reduce heat to medium-high and boil gently, uncovered, 3 to 4 minutes or until ravioli float to surface and are just tender. Remove to warm platter with slotted spoon. Repeat with remaining ravioli. Serve ravioli with Wild Mushroom Sauce and sprinkle with remaining ⅔ cup Parmesan cheese.

Makes 8 servings

Wild Mushroom Sauce

3 tablespoons olive oil
12 ounces shiitake or porcini
    mushrooms, sliced
6 ounces cremini or button mushrooms,
    sliced
1½ cups sliced green onions and tops
1 tablespoon dried basil leaves
½ to 1 teaspoon dried thyme leaves
3 cups vegetable broth, divided
1½ tablespoons cornstarch
2 tablespoons minced parsley
½ teaspoon salt
4 to 6 dashes hot pepper sauce

Heat oil in large skillet over medium heat until hot. Add mushrooms, green onions, basil and thyme; cook and stir 5 minutes or until mushrooms release liquid. Continue cooking 10 minutes or until mushrooms have darkened and all liquid is evaporated, stirring occasionally. Add 2¾ cups broth; bring to a boil. Reduce heat to medium-low and simmer, uncovered, 10 to 12 minutes or until broth is reduced by one-third. Return liquid to a boil.

Combine cornstarch and remaining ¼ cup broth in small cup. Add to mushroom mixture. Boil, stirring constantly, 1 to 2 minutes or until thickened. Stir in parsley, salt and pepper sauce.

Makes about 3 cups

Cheese Ravioli with Wild Mushroom Sauce

Broccoli Lasagna Bianca

1 (15- to 16-ounce) container fat-free
  ricotta cheese
1 cup EGG BEATERS® Healthy Real
  Egg Product
1 tablespoon minced basil (or
  1 teaspoon dried basil leaves)
½ cup chopped onion
1 clove garlic, minced
2 tablespoons FLEISCHMANN'S®
  Margarine
¼ cup all-purpose flour
2 cups skim milk
2 (10-ounce) packages frozen chopped
  broccoli, thawed and well drained
1 cup (4 ounces) shredded part-skim
  mozzarella cheese
9 lasagna noodles, cooked and drained
1 small tomato, chopped
2 tablespoons grated Parmesan cheese
  Fresh basil leaves, for garnish

In medium bowl, combine ricotta cheese,
Egg Beaters® and minced basil; set aside.

In large saucepan, over medium heat, sauté
onion and garlic in margarine until tender-
crisp. Stir in flour; cook for 1 minute.
Gradually stir in milk; cook, stirring until
mixture thickens and begins to boil. Remove
from heat; stir in broccoli and mozzarella
cheese.

In lightly greased 13×9×2-inch baking
dish, place 3 lasagna noodles; top with
⅓ each ricotta and broccoli mixtures. Repeat
layers 2 more times. Top with tomato;
sprinkle with Parmesan cheese. Bake at
350°F for 1 hour or until set. Let stand
10 minutes before serving. Garnish with
basil leaves.   *Makes 8 servings*

Fettuccine with Sun-Dried Tomato Cream

⅔ cup sun-dried tomatoes
3 to 4 cloves garlic
1 (8-ounce) container
  PHILADELPHIA BRAND® Soft
  Cream Cheese
½ teaspoon dried oregano leaves,
  crushed
¼ cup butter or margarine
¼ cup BREAKSTONE'S® Sour Cream
1 pound fettuccine, cooked, drained,
  kept warm
¼ cup olive oil
  Salt and pepper
2 tablespoons chopped fresh parsley

• Cover tomatoes with boiling water; let
stand 10 minutes. Drain.

• Place tomatoes and garlic in food
processor or blender container; process until
coarsely chopped. Add cream cheese and
oregano; process until well blended.

• Melt butter in medium saucepan; stir in
cream cheese mixture and sour cream. Cook
until thoroughly heated.

• Toss warm fettuccine with oil.

• Add cream cheese mixture. Season to taste
with salt and pepper. Sprinkle with chopped
parsley. Serve immediately.
      Makes 8 to 10 servings

Broccoli Lasagna Bianca

Stuffed Jumbo Shells with Garlic Vegetables

Garlic Vegetables (recipe follows)
12 jumbo pasta shells
2 cups ricotta cheese
1 package (10 ounces) frozen chopped
    spinach, thawed and squeezed dry
¼ cup plus 2 tablespoons grated
    Parmesan cheese, divided
2 cloves garlic, minced
¾ teaspoon dried marjoram leaves
½ to 1 teaspoon salt
½ teaspoon dried basil leaves
½ teaspoon ground black pepper
¼ teaspoon dried thyme leaves

Prepare Garlic Vegetables. Spoon into 10-inch round baking dish.

Preheat oven to 350°F. Cook shells according to package directions. Drain and cool.

Combine ricotta, spinach, ¼ cup Parmesan cheese, garlic, marjoram, salt, basil, pepper and thyme in medium bowl. Spoon cheese mixture into shells. Arrange shells on top of Garlic Vegetables. Carefully spoon sauce from vegetables over shells.

Bake, loosely covered with foil, 35 to 40 minutes or until stuffed shells are heated through. Sprinkle remaining 2 tablespoons Parmesan cheese over shells.

Makes 4 servings

Garlic Vegetables

2 tablespoons olive oil, divided
1 large head garlic, peeled and coarsely
    chopped
⅓ cup sun-dried tomatoes (not packed
    in oil)
2 tablespoons all-purpose flour
1¼ cups canned vegetable broth
1 medium zucchini
1 medium yellow summer squash
2 large carrots, cut diagonally into
    ¼-inch slices
2 tablespoons minced fresh parsley
    Salt
    Ground black pepper

Heat 1 tablespoon oil in small skillet over medium heat until hot. Add garlic; cook and stir 2 to 3 minutes. Reduce heat to low and cook about 15 minutes or until garlic is golden brown, stirring frequently. Add tomatoes; cook over medium heat 2 minutes. Stir in flour. Cook and stir 2 minutes. Gradually stir in broth. Cook 1 to 2 minutes or until sauce thickens, stirring constantly.

Cut zucchini and squash lengthwise into halves. Cut each half into crosswise slices.

Heat remaining 1 tablespoon oil in medium skillet over medium heat until hot. Add carrots; cook and stir 2 minutes. Add zucchini and squash; cook and stir 3 minutes or until crisp-tender. Remove from heat. Stir garlic mixture and parsley into carrot mixture in skillet. Season to taste with salt and pepper.

Makes 2 cups

Stuffed Jumbo Shells with Garlic Vegetables

Roasted Vegetable Lasagne

12 lasagne noodles, uncooked
   Nonstick cooking spray
8 ounces mushrooms, halved
2 zucchini or yellow squash, halved
   lengthwise and cut crosswise into
   ½-inch pieces
2 yellow or red bell peppers, cut into
   1-inch pieces
1 small red onion, cut into 1-inch pieces
2 tablespoons balsamic vinegar
1 teaspoon olive or vegetable oil
2 cloves garlic, minced
½ teaspoon dried rosemary, crushed
1 (26-ounce) jar fat-free spaghetti sauce
1 (15-ounce) container part-skim
   ricotta cheese
1 (10-ounce) package frozen chopped
   spinach, thawed, squeezed dry
1 large egg white
¼ teaspoon hot red pepper flakes
1 cup shredded part-skim mozzarella
   cheese
¼ cup grated Parmesan cheese

Prepare lasagne according to package directions. While lasagne is cooking, heat oven to 425° F. Coat shallow metal roasting pan with cooking spray. Add mushrooms, squash, bell peppers and onion. In small dish, combine vinegar, oil, garlic and rosemary; brush evenly over vegetables. Bake vegetables 15 minutes; toss vegetables. Continue baking 8 to 10 minutes or until vegetables are browned and tender.

Spoon 1 cup spaghetti sauce over bottom of 13×9-inch baking dish. Arrange 4 pieces of lasagne (3 lengthwise, 1 crosswise) over sauce. Cover lasagne with 1 cup sauce. In medium bowl, combine ricotta cheese, spinach, egg white and hot red pepper flakes. Drop half of cheese mixture by spoonfuls over sauce; arrange half of roasted vegetables between spoonfuls of cheese mixture. Arrange another 4 pieces of lasagne over cheese and vegetables, pressing lightly;

top with 1 cup sauce. Repeat layering with remaining cheese, roasted vegetables, 4 pieces of lasagne and remaining sauce.

Reduce oven temperature to 375°F. Cover lasagne with foil; bake 45 minutes. Uncover; sprinkle with mozzarella and Parmesan cheeses; continue baking, uncovered, 5 minutes or until cheeses are melted. Let stand 10 minutes before serving.

Makes 8 servings

Favorite recipe from **National Pasta Association**

Roma Artichoke and Tomato Ragu

1¾ cups (14.5-ounce can) CONTADINA®
   Recipe Ready Diced Tomatoes,
   drained
1 cup (6-ounce jar) marinated
   artichoke hearts, sliced, undrained
¼ cup sliced ripe olives, drained
2 tablespoons chopped fresh parsley *or*
   2 teaspoons dried parsley flakes
2 tablespoons chopped fresh basil *or*
   2 teaspoons dried basil leaves,
   crushed
1 clove garlic, minced
¼ teaspoon salt
⅛ teaspoon ground black pepper

COMBINE tomatoes, artichoke hearts and juice, olives, parsley, basil, garlic, salt and pepper in large bowl.

COVER; chill for several hours to blend flavors.

TOSS with pasta or serve at room temperature on toasted Italian bread slices or pizza.
Makes 4 servings

Roma Artichoke and Tomato Ragu

Spicy Ravioli and Cheese

1 medium red bell pepper, thinly sliced
1 medium green bell pepper, thinly
    sliced
1 medium yellow bell pepper, thinly
    sliced
1 tablespoon olive or vegetable oil
½ teaspoon LAWRY'S® Seasoned Salt
¼ teaspoon LAWRY'S® Garlic Powder
    with Parsley
¼ teaspoon sugar
1 package (8 or 9 ounces) fresh or
    frozen ravioli
1½ cups chunky salsa
4 ounces mozzarella cheese, thinly
    sliced
2 green onions, sliced

Place bell peppers in broiler proof baking dish; sprinkle with oil, Seasoned Salt, Garlic Powder with Parsley and sugar. Broil 15 minutes or until tender and browned, turning once. Prepare ravioli according to package directions. Pour ¾ cup salsa in bottom of 8-inch square baking dish. Alternate layers of bell peppers, ravioli, cheese and green onions. Pour remaining ¾ cup salsa over layers. Cover with foil; bake in 350°F oven 15 to 20 minutes or until heated through and cheese melts.

Makes 4 to 6 servings

Linguine with Spinach Pesto

1 (10-ounce) package frozen chopped
    spinach, thawed and well drained
1 cup EGG BEATERS® Healthy Real
    Egg Product
⅓ cup PLANTERS® Walnut Pieces
¼ cup grated Parmesan cheese
2 cloves garlic, crushed
1 pound thin linguine, cooked in
    unsalted water and drained
½ cup diced red bell pepper
    Additional grated Parmesan cheese,
    optional

In electric blender container or food processor, blend spinach, Egg Beaters®, walnuts, ¼ cup cheese and garlic until smooth. Toss with hot linguine and bell pepper. Top with additional cheese if desired. *Makes 8 servings*

Fettuccine with Olive Pesto

10 ounces dried fettuccine
1½ cups whole pitted California Ripe
    Olives
3 tablespoons drained capers
4 teaspoons lemon juice
1 tablespoon olive oil
2 teaspoons Dijon mustard
2 to 3 cloves garlic, peeled
¼ cup finely chopped fresh basil
¼ cup grated Parmesan cheese
    Basil sprigs

Cook fettuccine according to package directions. While pasta cooks, combine olives, capers, lemon juice, oil, mustard and garlic in food processor or blender. Process until coarsely puréed. Stir in chopped basil and cheese; set aside. Drain pasta well and transfer to large warm serving bowl. Spoon pesto over pasta and mix gently. Garnish with basil sprigs. *Makes 4 servings*

Favorite recipe from **California Olive Industry**

Spicy Ravioli and Cheese

Main Dishes

Grilled Vegetable Kabobs

**1 large red or green bell pepper
1 large zucchini
1 large yellow squash or additional
    zucchini
12 ounces large mushrooms
2 tablespoons olive oil
2 tablespoons red wine vinegar
1 package (7.2 ounces) RICE-A-RONI®
    Herb & Butter
1 large tomato, chopped
¼ cup grated Parmesan cheese**

1. Cut red pepper into twelve 1-inch pieces. Cut zucchini and yellow squash crosswise into twelve ½-inch slices. Marinate red pepper, zucchini, yellow squash and mushrooms in combined oil and vinegar 15 minutes.

2. Alternately thread marinated vegetables onto 4 large skewers. Brush with any remaining oil mixture; set aside.

3. Prepare Rice-A-Roni® Mix as package directs.

4. While Rice-A-Roni® is simmering, grill kabobs over medium-low coals *or* broil 4 to 5 inches from heat 12 to 14 minutes or until tender and browned, turning once.

5. Stir tomato into rice. Serve rice topped with kabobs. Sprinkle with cheese.

Makes 4 servings

Viking Vegetable Cassoulet

**4 cups sliced mushrooms
2 tablespoons olive oil
2 large onions, thickly sliced
1 large clove garlic, minced
2 medium zucchini, cut into 1-inch
    pieces
1½ cups sliced yellow squash
2 cans (16 ounces each) white beans,
    drained
1 can (14½ ounces) plum tomatoes, cut
    up, with juice
⅓ cup chopped parsley
1 teaspoon dried basil, crushed
½ teaspoon dried oregano, crushed
½ cup bread crumbs
1 teaspoon butter, melted
2 cups (8 ounces) shredded
    JARLSBERG Cheese**

In large, deep skillet, brown mushrooms in oil. Add onions and garlic; sauté 5 minutes. Add zucchini and squash; sauté until vegetables are crisp-tender. Blend in beans, tomatoes, parsley, basil and oregano.

Spoon into 2-quart baking dish. Combine bread crumbs and butter in small bowl. Sprinkle bread crumbs around edge. Bake at 350°F 20 minutes. Top with cheese and bake 20 minutes longer.   *Makes 6 to 8 servings*

Grilled Vegetable Kabobs

Polenta with Vegetable Medley

Cheese Polenta (recipe follows)
1 tablespoon margarine or butter
2 teaspoons olive oil
1 medium fennel bulb with stalks, cored and cut into thin wedges
1 cup chopped onions
2 tablespoons snipped chives
½ teaspoon sugar
2 carrots, cut into julienned strips
4 ounces medium Brussels sprouts (6 to 8), cut into halves
½ to 1 cup canned vegetable broth
Salt
Black pepper

Prepare Cheese Polenta; set aside. Heat margarine and oil in large skillet over medium heat until butter melts. Add fennel. Cook 6 to 8 minutes or until lightly browned on both sides. Place in medium bowl. Add onions, chives and sugar to skillet. Cook and stir 5 minutes or until onions are tender. Return fennel to skillet. Add carrots, Brussels sprouts and ½ cup broth. Bring to a boil; reduce heat to low. Cover and simmer 15 to 20 minutes or until Brussels sprouts are tender, adding more broth if necessary to keep mixture moist. Season to taste with salt and pepper.

Spray large nonstick skillet with cooking spray. Heat over medium heat until hot. Cut Cheese Polenta into wedges. Cook 3 minutes per side or until browned. Place on serving plates; top with vegetable mixture. Garnish, if desired. *Makes 4 to 6 servings*

Cheese Polenta

1 cup cold water
1 cup yellow cornmeal
1½ cups boiling water
2 to 4 tablespoons crumbled Gorgonzola cheese
1 clove garlic, minced
1 teaspoon salt

Stir water into cornmeal in large saucepan. Heat over medium heat until warm. Slowly stir in boiling water. Bring to a boil over medium-high heat. Reduce heat to low. Cook 15 minutes or until mixture is thick, stirring constantly. Stir in cheese, garlic and salt. Pour into greased 8-inch round pan; let stand 10 minutes or until firm.
Makes 4 to 6 servings

Vegetarian Tofu Stir-Fry

1 block tofu
2 tablespoons vegetable oil
1 teaspoon minced fresh gingerroot
1 medium onion, chunked
⅛ teaspoon salt
6 ounces fresh snow peas, trimmed and cut diagonally in half
⅓ cup KIKKOMAN® Stir-Fry Sauce
2 medium-size fresh tomatoes, chunked
¼ cup slivered blanched almonds, toasted

Cut tofu into ½-inch cubes; drain well on several layers of paper towels. Heat oil in hot wok or large skillet over high heat. Add ginger; stir-fry 30 seconds, or until fragrant. Add onion and salt; stir-fry 2 minutes. Add snow peas; stir-fry 1 minute. Add stir-fry sauce, tomatoes and tofu. Gently stir to coat tofu and vegetables with sauce. Reduce heat and cook only until tomatoes and tofu are heated through. Sprinkle with almonds; serve immediately. *Makes 4 servings*

Polenta with Vegetable Medley

Basque Style Eggplant Casserole

6 tablespoons oil, divided
1 onion, cut into strips
2 green peppers, seeded and cut into strips
5 large mushrooms, sliced
1 celery stalk, sliced diagonally
5 cloves CHRISTOPHER RANCH Fresh Garlic, minced
6 tomatoes, peeled and diced
Salt to taste
1 tablespoon fines herbes
2 eggs
1 tablespoon water
1 large eggplant
½ cup freshly grated Parmesan cheese
1 cup shredded Swiss cheese

Heat 3 tablespoons oil in large skillet; add onion, green peppers, mushrooms, celery and garlic. Sauté until tender. Add tomatoes. Bring to a boil. Add salt and fines herbes. Turn heat to low and simmer sauce for 30 minutes. Beat eggs, water and pinch of salt. Peel eggplant and slice into large slices. Dip in egg mixture and fry eggplant in skillet with remaining oil until tender. Arrange eggplant slices in large baking dish. Sprinkle with Parmesan cheese. Pour tomato sauce over top and sprinkle with Swiss cheese. Heat in 350° oven until cheese is melted.

Eggplant Crêpes with Roasted Tomato Sauce

Eggplant Crêpes with Roasted Tomato Sauce

Roasted Tomato Sauce (recipe follows)
2 eggplants (about 8 to 9 inches long)
Nonstick olive oil cooking spray
1 package (10 ounces) frozen chopped spinach, thawed and pressed dry
1 cup ricotta cheese
½ cup grated Parmesan cheese
1¼ cups (5 ounces) shredded Gruyère* cheese
Fresh oregano leaves for garnish

*Gruyère cheese is a Swiss cheese that has been aged for 10 to 12 months. Any Swiss cheese may be substituted.

Prepare Roasted Tomato Sauce; set aside. *Reduce oven temperature to 425°F.*

Cut eggplants lengthwise into ¼-inch-thick slices. Arrange 18 of largest slices on nonstick baking sheets in single layer. Spray both sides of eggplant slices with cooking spray. (Reserve any remaining slices for other uses.) Bake eggplant 10 minutes; turn and bake 5 to 10 minutes more or until tender. Cool. *Reduce oven temperature to 350°F.*

Combine spinach, ricotta and Parmesan cheese; mix well. Spray 12×8-inch baking pan with cooking spray. Spread spinach mixture evenly on eggplant slices; roll up slices, beginning at short ends. Place rolls, seam side down, in baking dish. Cover dish with foil and bake 25 minutes. Uncover; sprinkle rolls with Gruyère cheese. Bake, uncovered, 5 minutes more or until cheese is melted. Serve with Roasted Tomato Sauce. Garnish, if desired. *Makes 4 to 6 servings*

Roasted Tomato Sauce

20 ripe plum tomatoes (about 2⅔ pounds), cut in half and seeded
3 tablespoons olive oil, divided
½ teaspoon salt
⅓ cup minced fresh basil
½ teaspoon ground black pepper

Preheat oven to 450°F. Toss tomatoes with 1 tablespoon oil and salt. Place, cut sides down, on nonstick baking sheet. Bake 20 to 25 minutes or until skins are blistered. Cool. Process tomatoes, remaining 2 tablespoons oil, basil and pepper in food processor until smooth. *Makes about 1 cup*

Low-Fat Chimichangas

1 (16-ounce) can black beans, rinsed and drained
1 (8-ounce) can stewed tomatoes
2 to 3 teaspoons chili powder
1 teaspoon dried oregano
22 to 24 corn tortillas (6-inch)
1 cup finely chopped green onions including tops
1½ cups (6 ounces) shredded JARLSBERG LITE™ Cheese

Mix beans, tomatoes, chili powder and oregano in medium saucepan. Cover and simmer 5 minutes. Uncover and simmer, stirring and crushing some of beans with wooden spoon, 5 minutes longer. Set aside. Warm tortillas according to package directions; keep warm. Place one tablespoon bean mixture on center of each tortilla. Sprinkle with rounded teaspoon onion, then rounded tablespoon cheese. Fold opposite sides of tortillas over mixture, forming square packets. Place folded sides down on nonstick skillet. Repeat until all ingredients are used. Cook, covered, over low heat 3 to 5 minutes until heated through and bottoms are crispy. Serve at once or keep warm on covered warming tray.

Makes 6 to 8 servings

Mu Shu Vegetables

Peanut Sauce (recipe follows)
3 tablespoons reduced-sodium soy
    sauce
2 tablespoons dry sherry
1½ tablespoons minced fresh ginger
2 teaspoons cornstarch
1½ teaspoons sesame oil
3 cloves garlic, minced
1 tablespoon peanut oil
3 leeks, washed and cut into 2-inch
    slivers
3 carrots, peeled and julienned
1 cup thinly sliced fresh shiitake
    mushrooms
1 small head Napa or Savoy cabbage,
    shredded (about 4 cups)
2 cups mung bean sprouts, rinsed and
    drained
8 ounces firm tofu, drained and cut into
    2½×¼-inch strips
12 flour tortillas (8-inch diameter),
    warmed*
¾ cup finely chopped honey roasted
    peanuts

Tortillas can be softened and warmed in microwave oven just before using. Stack tortillas and wrap in plastic wrap. Microwave on HIGH ½ to 1 minute, turning over and rotating ¼ turn once during heating.

Prepare Peanut Sauce; set aside. Combine soy sauce, sherry, ginger, cornstarch, sesame oil and garlic in small bowl until smooth; set aside.

Heat wok over medium-high heat 1 minute or until hot. Drizzle peanut oil into wok and heat 30 seconds. Add leeks, carrots and mushrooms; stir-fry 2 minutes. Add cabbage; stir-fry 3 minutes or until just tender. Add bean sprouts and tofu; stir-fry 1 minute or until hot. Stir soy sauce mixture and add to wok. Cook and stir 1 minute or until thickened.

Spread each tortilla with about 1 teaspoon Peanut Sauce. Spoon ½ cup vegetable mixture on bottom half of tortilla; sprinkle with 1 tablespoon peanuts.

Fold bottom edge of tortilla over filling; fold in side edges. Roll up to completely enclose filling. Or, spoon ½ cup vegetable mixture on one half of tortilla. Fold bottom edge over filling. Fold in one side edge. Serve with Peanut Sauce.   *Makes 6 servings*

Peanut Sauce

3 tablespoons sugar
3 tablespoons dry sherry
3 tablespoons reduced-sodium soy
    sauce
3 tablespoons water
2 teaspoons white wine vinegar
⅓ cup creamy peanut butter

Combine all ingredients except peanut butter in small saucepan. Bring to a boil over medium-high heat, stirring constantly. Boil 1 minute or until sugar melts. Stir in peanut butter until smooth; cool to room temperature.   *Makes ⅔ cup*

Mu Shu Vegetables

Cabbage-Cheese Strudel

1 tablespoon vegetable oil
1 cup chopped onions
½ cup sliced leeks
½ cup sliced button mushrooms
½ cup seeded and chopped tomato
¼ head green cabbage, shredded
1 cup broccoli florets, steamed
1½ teaspoons caraway seeds, crushed, divided
1 teaspoon dried dill weed
½ teaspoon salt
¼ teaspoon ground black pepper
1 package (8 ounces) cream cheese, softened
1 egg, beaten
¾ cup cooked brown rice
¾ cup (3 ounces) shredded Cheddar cheese
6 sheets frozen phyllo pastry, thawed
6 to 8 tablespoons margarine or butter, melted

Heat oil in large saucepan over medium heat until hot. Add onions and leeks; cook and stir 3 minutes. Add mushrooms and tomato; cook and stir 5 minutes. Add cabbage, broccoli, 1 teaspoon caraway seeds, dill weed, salt and pepper. Cover; cook over medium heat 8 to 10 minutes or until cabbage wilts. Remove cover; cook 10 minutes more or until cabbage is soft and beginning to brown.

Combine cream cheese, egg, rice and Cheddar cheese in medium bowl. Stir into cabbage mixture until blended.

Preheat oven to 375°F. Unroll phyllo dough. Cover with plastic wrap and damp, clean kitchen towel. Brush 1 phyllo dough sheet with margarine. Top with 2 more sheets, brushing each with margarine. Spoon half of cabbage mixture 2 inches from short end of phyllo. Spread mixture to cover about half of phyllo. Roll up dough from short end with filling. Place, seam side down, on greased cookie sheet. Flatten roll slightly with hands and brush with margarine. Repeat with remaining phyllo, margarine and cabbage mixture. Sprinkle tops of rolls with remaining ½ teaspoon caraway seeds.

Bake 45 to 50 minutes or until golden brown. Cool 10 minutes. Cut each roll diagonally into 3 pieces with serrated knife.

Makes 6 servings

Apple-Potato Pancakes

1¼ cups unpeeled, finely chopped apples
1 cup peeled, grated potatoes
½ cup MOTT'S® Natural Apple Sauce
½ cup all-purpose flour
2 egg whites
1 teaspoon salt
Additional MOTT'S® Natural Apple Sauce or apple slices (optional)

1. Preheat oven to 475°F. Spray cookie sheet with nonstick cooking spray.

2. In medium bowl, combine apples, potatoes, ½ cup apple sauce, flour, egg whites and salt.

3. Spray large nonstick skillet with nonstick cooking spray; heat over medium heat until hot. Drop rounded tablespoonfuls of batter 2 inches apart into skillet. Cook 2 to 3 minutes on each side or until lightly browned. Place pancakes on prepared cookie sheet.

4. Bake 10 to 15 minutes or until crisp. Serve with additional apple sauce or apple slices, if desired. Refrigerate leftovers.

Makes 12 servings

Cabbage-Cheese Strudel

Rice Cakes with Mushroom Walnut Ragoût

⅔ cup Arborio rice
1 egg
1 egg white
½ cup grated Parmesan cheese
3 tablespoons minced green onions
1 ounce dried porcini mushrooms
1 cup boiling water
1 tablespoon olive oil
1 medium onion, sliced
2 cloves garlic, minced
8 ounces button mushrooms, sliced
1 teaspoon dried oregano
1 can (14½ ounces) tomato wedges,
    undrained
2 teaspoons lemon juice
½ teaspoon ground black pepper
¼ teaspoon salt
⅓ cup chopped toasted walnuts
    Asiago or Parmesan cheese shavings

Cook rice according to package directions. Cool.

Preheat oven to 350°F. Spray 8-inch square baking pan with nonstick cooking spray. Beat egg and egg white in medium bowl until blended. Add rice, grated Parmesan and green onions; mix well. Press into prepared pan. Bake 20 to 25 minutes or until set.

Soak dried mushrooms in boiling water in small bowl 15 to 20 minutes or until soft. Drain, reserving liquid. Chop mushrooms. Heat oil in large nonstick skillet over medium heat until hot. Add onion and garlic; cook and stir 5 minutes. Add fresh mushrooms, dried mushrooms and oregano; cook and stir 5 minutes or until fresh mushrooms are tender.

Drain tomatoes, reserving ¼ cup juice. Add tomatoes, reserved juice, reserved mushroom liquid, lemon juice, pepper and salt to skillet. Bring to a boil. Reduce heat to low. Simmer, uncovered, 15 minutes or until sauce thickens. Stir in walnuts.

Cut Rice Cakes into 8 rectangles. Top with ragoût; sprinkle cheese shavings over ragoût.

Makes 4 servings

Vegetable Stuffed Peppers

1 small zucchini, quartered lengthwise
    and cut into ¼-inch slices
1 cup quartered fresh mushrooms
½ cup chopped onion
1 clove garlic, minced
1 teaspoon olive oil
1 can (15 ounces) cannelini or navy
    beans, drained
1 fresh tomato, chopped
1 cup cooked rice
¾ cup HEINZ® Tomato Ketchup
½ cup tomato sauce
¼ cup plus 2 tablespoons grated
    Parmesan cheese, divided
1 teaspoon dried basil leaves
½ teaspoon salt
¼ teaspoon dried oregano leaves
3 medium red, yellow or green bell
    peppers, cut lengthwise and seeded

Spray 2-quart oblong baking dish with nonstick cooking spray. In large skillet, sauté zucchini, mushrooms, onion and garlic in oil until vegetables are crisp-tender, stirring frequently. Add beans, tomato, rice, ketchup, tomato sauce, ¼ cup Parmesan cheese, basil, salt and oregano; mix well. Spoon vegetable mixture into pepper halves; place in prepared baking dish. Cover; bake in 375°F oven 35 minutes. Uncover; baste with pan juices. Sprinkle each pepper with 1 teaspoon Parmesan cheese. Bake an additional 20 minutes or until filling is hot.

Makes 6 servings

Rice Cakes with Mushroom Walnut Ragoût

Broccoli-Tofu Stir-Fry

2 cups rice
1 can (about 14 ounces) vegetable broth, divided
3 tablespoons cornstarch
1 tablespoon reduced-sodium soy sauce
½ teaspoon sugar
¼ teaspoon sesame oil
1 package (16 ounces) extra-firm tofu
1 teaspoon peanut oil
1 tablespoon minced fresh ginger
3 cloves garlic, minced
3 cups broccoli florets
2 cups sliced mushrooms
½ cup chopped green onions
1 large red bell pepper, seeded and cut into strips
Prepared Szechuan sauce (optional)

1. Cook rice according to package directions. Combine ¼ cup vegetable broth, cornstarch, soy sauce, sugar and sesame oil in small bowl until well blended. Drain tofu; cut into 1-inch cubes.

2. Heat peanut oil in large nonstick wok or skillet over medium heat until hot. Add ginger and garlic. Cook and stir 5 minutes. Add remaining vegetable broth, broccoli, mushrooms, green onions and bell pepper. Cook and stir over medium-high heat 5 minutes or until vegetables are crisp-tender. Add tofu; cook 2 minutes, stirring occasionally. Stir cornstarch mixture; add to vegetable mixture. Cook and stir until sauce thickens. Serve over rice with Szechuan sauce, if desired. Garnish as desired.

Makes 6 servings

Refried Bean Tostadas

1¾ cups (1-pound can) ORTEGA® Refried Beans
¼ cup chopped onion
1 package (1¼ ounces) ORTEGA® Taco Seasoning Mix
1 package (10) ORTEGA® Tostada Shells
2 cups shredded lettuce
½ cup (2 ounces) shredded Cheddar cheese
⅓ cup sliced ripe olives
2 medium ripe avocados, seeded, peeled, cut into 20 slices
¾ cup ORTEGA® Thick & Smooth Taco Sauce, hot, medium or mild

COMBINE beans, onion and taco seasoning mix in medium saucepan. Cook, stirring frequently, for 4 to 5 minutes or until heated through.

REMOVE tostada shells from freshness pack. Heat shells in microwave oven on HIGH for 40 to 60 seconds or place on baking sheet in preheated 350°F. oven for 5 to 6 minutes.

SPREAD ¼ cup bean mixture over each shell. Top with cheese, lettuce, olives, avocado and taco sauce.

Makes 10 servings

Refried Bean Tostadas

Torta Rustica

1 package active dry yeast
1 teaspoon sugar
1 cup warm water (105° to 115°F)
3 cups plus 2 tablespoons all-purpose flour, divided
1½ teaspoons salt, divided
3 tablespoons vegetable oil, divided
1½ teaspoons dried basil leaves, divided
1½ cups chopped onions
1 cup chopped carrots
2 cloves garlic, minced
2 medium zucchini, cubed
½ pound button mushrooms, sliced
1 can (16 ounces) whole tomatoes, undrained and chopped
1 can (15 ounces) artichoke hearts, drained and cut into halves
1 medium red bell pepper, seeded and cut into 1-inch squares
½ teaspoon dried oregano leaves
¼ teaspoon ground black pepper
2 cups (8 ounces) shredded provolone or mozzarella cheese

Sprinkle yeast and sugar over warm water in small bowl; stir until yeast is dissolved. Let stand 5 minutes or until mixture is bubbly. Combine 3 cups flour and 1 teaspoon salt in food processor. With food processor running, add yeast mixture, 2 tablespoons oil and ½ teaspoon basil. Process until mixture forms dough that leaves side of bowl, adding additional water or flour 1 tablespoon at a time if necessary. *Dough will be sticky.* Place dough in large greased bowl; turn dough over. Cover with towel; let rise in warm place about 1 hour or until doubled in bulk.

Heat remaining 1 tablespoon oil in large saucepan over medium heat until hot. Add onions, carrots and garlic; cook and stir 5 minutes or until onions are tender. Stir in zucchini, mushrooms, tomatoes, artichoke hearts, bell pepper, remaining 1 teaspoon basil, oregano, remaining ½ teaspoon salt and black pepper. Bring to a boil over high heat. Reduce heat to low. Cover and simmer 10 minutes.

Punch down dough. Knead dough on lightly floured surface 1 minute. Cover with towel; let rest 10 minutes.

Preheat oven to 400°F. Grease 2-quart casserole or soufflé dish. Roll two thirds of dough on lightly floured surface to ½-inch thickness. Ease dough into casserole, allowing dough to extend 1 inch over edge. Spoon half of vegetable mixture into casserole. Sprinkle with 1 cup cheese. Repeat layers. Roll remaining dough on lightly floured surface into circle 2 inches larger than top of casserole; cut decorative designs in top of dough with paring knife. Place dough over filling. Fold edges of top dough over bottom dough; pinch with fingertips to seal edges.

Bake 30 to 35 minutes or until crust is golden brown, covering edge of dough with foil if necessary to prevent over browning.

Makes 6 servings

Spaghetti Squash Primavera

Spaghetti Squash Primavera

  2 teaspoons vegetable oil
½ teaspoon finely chopped garlic
¼ cup finely chopped red onion
¼ cup thinly sliced carrot
¼ cup thinly sliced red bell pepper
¼ cup thinly sliced green bell pepper
  1 can (14½ ounces) Italian-style stewed
     tomatoes
½ cup thinly sliced yellow squash
½ cup thinly sliced zucchini
½ cup frozen corn, thawed
½ teaspoon dried oregano leaves
⅛ teaspoon dried thyme leaves
  1 spaghetti squash (about 2 pounds)
  4 teaspoons grated Parmesan cheese
     (optional)
  2 tablespoons finely chopped fresh
     parsley

1. Heat oil in large skillet over medium-high heat until hot. Add garlic. Cook and stir 3 minutes. Add onion, carrot and peppers. Cook and stir 3 minutes. Add tomatoes, squash, zucchini, corn, oregano and thyme. Cook 5 minutes or until heated through, stirring occasionally.

2. Cut squash lengthwise in half. Remove seeds. Cover with plastic wrap. Microwave at HIGH 9 minutes or until squash separates easily into strands when tested with fork.

3. Cut each squash half lengthwise in half; separate strands with fork. Spoon vegetables evenly over squash. Top servings evenly with cheese, if desired, and parsley before serving.   *Makes 4 servings*

Acknowledgements

*The publishers would like to thank the companies and organizations listed
below for the use of their recipes and photos in this publication.*

Alpine Lace Brands, Inc.
American Italian Pasta Company
Black-Eyed Pea Jamboree—Athens, Texas
California Apricot Advisory Board
California Olive Industry
California Wild Rice
Christopher Ranch Garlic
Cucina Classica Italiana, Inc.
Filippo Berio Olive Oil
Golden Grain/Mission Pasta
Guiltless Gourmet, Inc.
Healthy Choice®
Heinz U.S.A.
The HVR Company
Kikkoman International Inc.
Kraft Foods, Inc.
Lawry's® Foods, Inc.
Lipton
McIlhenny Company
Minnesota Cultivated Wild Rice Council
MOTT'S® Inc., a division of Cadbury Beverages Inc.
Nabisco, Inc.
National Pasta Association
National Sunflower Association
Nestlé Food Company
Norseland, Inc.
North Dakota Barley Council
The Procter & Gamble Company
The Quaker® Oatmeal Kitchens
Sargento Foods Inc.®
South Texas Onion Committe
USA Rice Council
Walnut Marketing Board
Wisconsin Milk Marketing Board

Index

A
Apple-Potato Pancakes, 82
Apricot Couscous Pilaf, 54
Artichoke Hearts
    Artichoke Heart, Olive and Goat
        Cheese Pizza, 20
    Italian Garden Fusilli, 58
    Mediterranean Pita Sandwiches, 27
    Roma Artichoke and Tomato Ragu, 70
    Torta Rustica, 88
Asparagus
    Asparagus Pie, 34
    Asparagus-Swiss Souffle, 32
    Tortellini Asparagus Salad, 17
Avocados
    Meatless Muffaletta Sandwich, 26
    Pita in the Morning, 37
    Refried Bean Tostadas, 86

B
Barley
    Black Bean-and-Barley Salad, 44
    Greens, White Bean and Barley Soup,
        10
    Pearls o' Barley Salad, 45
    Tex-Mex Barley Bake, 40
Basic Crepês, 37
Basque Style Eggplant Casserole, 78
Beans
    Bean Salad with Bulgur, 47
    Black Bean-and-Barley Salad, 44
    Brown Rice Black Bean Burrito, 48
    Chunky Vegetable Chili, 13
    Glorious Garbanzo Salad, 50
    Greens, White Bean and Barley Soup,
        10
    Hearty Vegetable Gumbo, 15
    Italian Garden Fusilli, 58
    Louisiana Red Beans & Rice, 53
    Low-Fat Chimichangas, 79
    Meatless Sloppy Joes, 29
    Mediterranean Pita Sandwiches, 27
    Mexican Deep Dish Pizza, 24
    Refried Bean Tostadas, 86
    Tex-Mex Barley Bake, 40
    Vegetable Stuffed Peppers, 84
    Viking Vegetable Cassoulet, 74
Black Bean-and-Barley Salad, 44
Breakfast Burritos with Tomato-Basil
    Topping, 30
Broccoli
    Broccoli and Cauliflower Linguine, 63
    Broccoli Lasagna Bianca, 66
    Broccoli-Tofu Stir-Fry, 86
    Cabbage-Cheese Strudel, 82

Curried Vegetables, 54
Triple-Decker Vegetable Omelet, 38
Vegetable Calzone, 27
Brown Rice Black Bean Burrito, 48
Brown Rice Primavera, 50
Bulgur
    Bean Salad with Bulgur, 47
    Eggplant Bulgur Casserole, 42
    Tabbouleh, 48

C
Cabbage-Cheese Strudel, 82
California Veggie Rolls, 27
Casseroles
    Basque Style Eggplant Casserole, 78
    Broccoli Lasagna Bianca, 66
    Chile Tortilla Brunch Casserole, 38
    Eggplant Bulgur Casserole, 42
    Eggplant Crepês with Roasted Tomato
        Sauce, 79
    Hearty Manicotti, 56
    Mexicali Wild Rice Casserole, 47
    Roasted Vegetable Lasagne, 70
    Spicy Ravioli and Cheese, 72
    Stuffed Jumbo Shells with Garlic
        Vegetables, 68
    Tex-Mex Barley Bake, 40
    Torta Rustica, 88
    Vegetable Stuffed Peppers, 84
    Viking Vegetable Cassoulet, 74
Cauliflower
    Broccoli and Cauliflower Linguine, 63
    Encore Salad, 48
Cheese
    Artichoke Heart, Olive and Goat
        Cheese Pizza, 20
    Asparagus Pie, 34
    Asparagus-Swiss Souffle, 32
    Basque Style Eggplant Casserole, 78
    Black Bean-and-Barley Salad, 44
    Breakfast Burritos with Tomato-Basil
        Topping, 30
    Broccoli and Cauliflower Linguine, 63
    Broccoli Lasagna Bianca, 66
    Brown Rice Black Bean Burrito, 48
    Cabbage-Cheese Strudel, 82
    California Veggie Rolls, 27
    Cheese Blintzes, 37
    Cheese Polenta, 76
    Cheese Ravioli with Wild Mushroom
        Sauce, 65
    Cheesy Salsa Omelet, 35
    Chile Tortilla Brunch Casserole, 38
    Double Onion Quiche, 30
    Easy Greek Salad, 12

Eggplant & Pepper Cheese
    Sandwiches, 22
Eggplant Bulgur Casserole, 42
Eggplant Crepês with Roasted Tomato
    Sauce, 79
Festive Focaccia Pizza Bread, 29
Fettuccine with Olive Pesto, 72
Fettuccine with Sun-Dried Tomato
    Cream, 66
Fresh Vegetable Pizza, 22
Glorious Garbanzo Salad, 50
Grilled Vegetable Kabobs, 74
Hearty Manicotti, 56
Italian Garden Fusilli, 58
Lentils, Olives and Feta, 53
Linguine with Spinach Pesto, 72
Low-Fat Chimichangas, 79
Meatless Muffaletta Sandwich, 26
Mediterranean Couscous, 45
Mexicali Wild Rice Casserole, 47
Mexican Deep Dish Pizza, 24
Pasta with Onions and Goat Cheese, 56
Pasta with Spinach-Cheese Sauce, 58
Pearls o' Barley Salad, 45
Penne with Tomatoes, Basil Leaves
    and Blue Cheese, 62
Pita in the Morning, 37
Porcini Mushroom Penne Rigate with
    Garlic Butter Sauce, 60
Refried Bean Tostadas, 86
Rice Cakes with Mushroom Walnut
    Ragoût, 84
Roasted Vegetable Lasagne, 70
Spaghetti Squash Primavera, 89
Spicy Ravioli and Cheese, 72
Spinach and Strawberry Salad with
    Wisconsin Gouda, 15
Stuffed Jumbo Shells with Garlic
    Vegetables, 68
Tex-Mex Barley Bake, 40
Texas Onion Pepper Tart, 32
Three-Pepper Risotto, 50
Torta Rustica, 88
Triple-Decker Vegetable Omelet, 38
Vegetable Calzone, 27
Vegetable Risotto, 42
Vegetable Stuffed Peppers, 84
Viking Vegetable Cassoulet, 74
Winter Pear and Stilton Salad, 8
Cheesy Salsa Omelet, 35
Chile Tortilla Brunch Casserole, 38
Chilled Potato Cucumber Soup with
    Roasted Red Pepper Swirl, 16
Chunky Vegetable Chili, 13
Cool Italian Tomato Soup, 18

Corn
    Brown Rice Black Bean Burrito, 48
    Chunky Vegetable Chili, 13
    Mexicali Wild Rice Casserole, 47
    Mexican Deep Dish Pizza, 24
    Roasted Corn & Wild Rice Salad, 40
    Spaghetti Squash Primavera, 89
Couscous
    Apricot Couscous Pilaf, 54
    Mediterranean Couscous, 45
Cream of Pumpkin Curry Soup, 18
Cucumbers
    Chilled Potato Cucumber Soup with
        Roasted Red Pepper Swirl, 16
    Cool Italian Tomato Soup, 18
    Easy Greek Salad, 12
    Mediterranean Pita Sandwiches, 27
    Pearls o' Barley Salad, 45
    Tabbouleh, 48
    Tuscan Summer Salad, 18
Curried Vegetables, 54
Curried Wild Rice Soup, 12

D
Double Onion Quiche, 30

E
Easy Greek Salad, 12
Eggplant
    Basque Style Eggplant Casserole, 78
    Eggplant & Pepper Cheese
        Sandwiches, 22
    Eggplant Bulgur Casserole, 42
    Eggplant Crepês with Roasted Tomato
        Sauce, 79
Eggs
    Asparagus Pie, 34
    Asparagus-Swiss Souffle, 32
    Breakfast Burritos with Tomato-Basil
        Topping, 30
    Broccoli Lasagna Bianca, 66
    Cheesy Salsa Omelet, 35
    Chile Tortilla Brunch Casserole, 38
    Double Onion Quiche, 30
    Light Farmhouse Frittata, 34
    Linguine with Spinach Pesto, 72
    Pita in the Morning, 37
    Scrambled Eggs Piperade, 34
    Texas Onion Pepper Tart, 32
    Triple-Decker Vegetable Omelet, 38
Encore Salad, 48

F
Festive Focaccia Pizza Bread, 29
Fettuccine with Olive Pesto, 72
Fettuccine with Sun-Dried Tomato
    Cream, 66
French Lentil Salad, 51
Fresh Vegetable Pizza, 22

G
Garlic Vegetables, 68
Glorious Garbanzo Salad, 50
Greens, White Bean and Barley Soup, 10
Grilled Vegetable Kabobs, 74

H
Hearty Manicotti, 56
Hearty Vegetable Gumbo, 15

I
Italian Garden Fusilli, 58

L
Lentils
    French Lentil Salad, 51
    Lentils, Olives and Feta, 53
Light Farmhouse Frittata, 34
Linguine with Spinach Pesto, 72
Linguine with Sun-Dried Tomato Pesto, 60
Louisiana Red Beans & Rice, 53
Low-Fat Chimichangas, 79

M
Meatless Muffaletta Sandwich, 26
Meatless Sloppy Joes, 29
Mediterranean Couscous, 45
Mediterranean Pita Sandwiches, 27
Mexicali Wild Rice Casserole, 47
Mexican Deep Dish Pizza, 24
Mu Shu Vegetables, 81
Mushrooms
    Basque Style Eggplant Casserole, 78
    Broccoli-Tofu Stir-Fry, 86
    Cabbage-Cheese Strudel, 82
    Cheesy Salsa Omelet, 35
    Curried Wild Rice Soup, 12
    Fresh Vegetable Pizza, 22
    Greens, White Bean and Barley Soup,
        10
    Grilled Vegetable Kabobs, 74
    Mu Shu Vegetables, 81
    Porcini Mushroom Penne Rigate with
        Garlic Butter Sauce, 60
    Rice Cakes with Mushroom Walnut
        Ragout, 84
    Roasted Vegetable Lasagne, 70
    Torta Rustica, 88
    Vegetable Risotto, 42
    Vegetable Stuffed Peppers, 84
    Viking Vegetable Cassoulet, 74
    Warm Mushroom Salad, 13
    Wild Mushroom Sauce, 65

N
New York-Style Pizza Crust, 20
Nuts
    Curried Vegetables, 54
    Festive Focaccia Pizza Bread, 29
    French Lentil Salad, 51
    Glorious Garbanzo Salad, 50
    Light Farmhouse Frittata, 34
    Linguine with Spinach Pesto, 72
    Mu Shu Vegetables, 81
    Peanut Sauce, 81
    Rice Cakes with Mushroom Walnut
        Ragoût, 84
    Spinach and Strawberry Salad with
        Wisconsin Gouda, 15
    Thai Pasta Salad with Peanut Sauce, 8
    Vegetarian Tofu Stir-Fry, 76

O
Olives
    Artichoke Heart, Olive and Goat
        Cheese Pizza, 20
    Easy Greek Salad, 12
    Encore Salad, 48
    Festive Focaccia Pizza Bread, 29
    Fettuccine with Olive Pesto, 72
    Lentils, Olives and Feta, 53
    Meatless Muffaletta Sandwich, 26
    Mediterranean Couscous, 45
    Mexican Deep Dish Pizza, 24
    Pearls o' Barley Salad, 45
    Refried Bean Tostadas, 86
    Roma Artichoke and Tomato Ragu, 70
    Tex-Mex Barley Bake, 40
    Tuscan Summer Salad, 18

P
Papaya-Kiwifruit Salad with Orange
    Dressing, 15
Pasta
    Broccoli and Cauliflower Linguine, 63
    Broccoli Lasagna Bianca, 66
    Cheese Ravioli with Wild Mushroom
        Sauce, 65
    Fettuccine with Olive Pesto, 72
    Fettuccine with Sun-Dried Tomato
        Cream, 66
    Hearty Manicotti, 56
    Italian Garden Fusilli, 58
    Linguine with Spinach Pesto, 72
    Linguine with Sun-Dried Tomato
        Pesto, 60
    Pasta with Onions and Goat Cheese,
        56
    Pasta with Spinach-Cheese Sauce, 58
    Penne with Tomatoes, Basil Leaves
        and Blue Cheese, 62
    Pennini with Vegetable Sauce
        "Springtime," 60
    Porcini Mushroom Penne Rigate with
        Garlic Butter Sauce, 60
    Roasted Vegetable Lasagne, 70
    Roma Artichoke and Tomato Ragu,
        70
    Spicy Ravioli and Cheese, 72
    Stuffed Jumbo Shells with Garlic
        Vegetables, 68
    Thai Pasta Salad with Peanut Sauce, 8
    Tortellini Asparagus Salad, 17
    Vegetable Lo Mein, 63
Peanut Sauce, 81
Pearls o' Barley Salad, 45
Peas
    Encore Salad, 48
    Italian Garden Fusilli, 58
    Pennini with Vegetable Sauce
        "Springtime," 60
    Vegetable Risotto, 42
    Vegetarian Tofu Stir-Fry, 76
Penne with Tomatoes, Basil Leaves and
    Blue Cheese, 62
Pennini with Vegetable Sauce
    "Springtime," 60

Peppers
Apricot Couscous Pilaf, 54
Basque Style Eggplant Casserole, 78
Broccoli-Tofu Stir-Fry, 86
Brown Rice Primavera, 50
Cool Italian Tomato Soup, 18
Curried Vegetables, 54
Eggplant & Pepper Cheese Sandwiches, 22
Eggplant Bulgur Casserole, 42
Encore Salad, 48
Grilled Vegetable Kabobs, 74
Hearty Vegetable Gumbo, 15
Light Farmhouse Frittata, 34
Linguine with Spinach Pesto, 72
Louisiana Red Beans & Rice, 53
Meatless Sloppy Joes, 29
Mediterranean Couscous, 45
Mexican Deep Dish Pizza, 24
Pennini with Vegetable Sauce "Springtime," 60
Roasted Corn & Wild Rice Salad, 40
Roasted Red Pepper Swirl, 16
Roasted Vegetable Lasagne, 70
Roasted Winter Vegetable Soup, 10
Scrambled Eggs Piperade, 34
Spaghetti Squash Primavera, 89
Spicy Ravioli and Cheese, 72
Spinach and Tomato Tofu Toss, 29
Tex-Mex Barley Bake, 40
Texas Onion Pepper Tart, 32
Three-Pepper Risotto, 50
Torta Rustica, 88
Tortellini Asparagus Salad, 17
Triple-Decker Vegetable Omelet, 38
Tuscan Summer Salad, 18
Vegetable Stuffed Peppers, 84
Pita in the Morning, 37
Pizzas
Artichoke Heart, Olive and Goat Cheese Pizza, 20
Festive Focaccia Pizza Bread, 29
Fresh Vegetable Pizza, 22
Mexican Deep Dish Pizza, 24
Vegetable Calzone, 27
Polenta with Vegetable Medley, 76
Porcini Mushroom Penne Rigate with Garlic Butter Sauce, 60
Potatoes
Apple-Potato Pancakes, 82
Breakfast Burritos with Tomato-Basil Topping, 30
Chilled Potato Cucumber Soup with Roasted Red Pepper Swirl, 16
Roasted Winter Vegetable Soup, 10

R
Refried Bean Tostadas, 86
Rice
Broccoli-Tofu Stir-Fry, 86
Brown Rice Black Bean Burrito, 48
Brown Rice Primavera, 50
Cabbage-Cheese Strudel, 82
Curried Vegetables, 54

Curried Wild Rice Soup, 12
Grilled Vegetable Kabobs, 74
Hearty Vegetable Gumbo, 15
Louisiana Red Beans & Rice, 53
Mexicali Wild Rice Casserole, 47
Rice Cakes with Mushroom Walnut Ragoût, 84
Roasted Corn & Wild Rice Salad, 40
Three-Pepper Risotto, 50
Vegetable Risotto, 42
Vegetable Stuffed Peppers, 84
Roasted Corn & Wild Rice Salad, 40
Roasted Red Pepper Swirl, 16
Roasted Tomato Sauce, 79
Roasted Vegetable Lasagne, 70
Roasted Winter Vegetable Soup, 10
Roma Artichoke and Tomato Ragu, 70

S
Salads
Bean Salad with Bulgur, 47
Black Bean-and-Barley Salad, 44
Easy Greek Salad, 12
Encore Salad, 48
French Lentil Salad, 51
Glorious Garbanzo Salad, 50
Papaya-Kiwifruit Salad with Orange Dressing, 15
Pearls o' Barley Salad, 45
Roasted Corn & Wild Rice Salad, 40
Spinach and Strawberry Salad with Wisconsin Gouda, 15
Thai Pasta Salad with Peanut Sauce, 8
Tortellini Asparagus Salad, 17
Tuscan Summer Salad, 18
Warm Mushroom Salad, 13
Winter Pear and Stilton Salad, 8
Sandwiches
California Veggie Rolls, 27
Eggplant & Pepper Cheese Sandwiches, 22
Meatless Muffaletta Sandwich, 26
Meatless Sloppy Joes, 29
Mediterranean Pita Sandwiches, 27
Spinach and Tomato Tofu Toss, 29
Scrambled Eggs Piperade, 34
Soups
Chilled Potato Cucumber Soup with Roasted Red Pepper Swirl, 16
Cool Italian Tomato Soup, 18
Cream of Pumpkin Curry Soup, 18
Curried Wild Rice Soup, 12
Greens, White Bean and Barley Soup, 10
Roasted Winter Vegetable Soup, 10
Vegetable Stock, 16
Spaghetti Squash Primavera, 89
Spicy Ravioli and Cheese, 72
Spinach
California Veggie Rolls, 27
Eggplant Crepês with Roasted Tomato Sauce, 79
Hearty Manicotti, 56
Lentils, Olives and Feta, 53
Linguine with Spinach Pesto, 72

Pasta with Spinach-Cheese Sauce, 58
Roasted Vegetable Lasagne, 70
Spinach and Strawberry Salad with Wisconsin Gouda, 15
Spinach and Tomato Tofu Toss, 29
Stuffed Jumbo Shells with Garlic Vegetables, 68
Tortellini Asparagus Salad, 17
Squash
Brown Rice Primavera, 50
Cream of Pumpkin Curry Soup, 18
Fresh Vegetable Pizza, 22
Garlic Vegetables, 68
Grilled Vegetable Kabobs, 74
Italian Garden Fusilli, 58
Pennini with Vegetable Sauce "Springtime," 60
Roasted Vegetable Lasagne, 70
Roasted Winter Vegetable Soup, 10
Spaghetti Squash Primavera, 89
Torta Rustica, 88
Vegetable Risotto, 42
Vegetable Stuffed Peppers, 84
Viking Vegetable Cassoulet, 74
Stuffed Jumbo Shells with Garlic Vegetables, 68

T
Tabbouleh, 48
Tex-Mex Barley Bake, 40
Texas Onion Pepper Tart, 32
Thai Pasta Salad with Peanut Sauce, 8
Thick Pizza Crust, 24
Three-Pepper Risotto, 50
Tofu
Broccoli-Tofu Stir-Fry, 86
Cheese Ravioli with Wild Mushroom Sauce, 65
Mu Shu Vegetables, 81
Spinach and Tomato Tofu Toss, 29
Vegetable Lo Mein, 63
Vegetarian Tofu Stir-Fry, 76
Torta Rustica, 88
Tortellini Asparagus Salad, 17
Triple-Decker Vegetable Omelet, 38
Tuscan Summer Salad, 18

V
Vegetable Calzone, 27
Vegetable Lo Mein, 63
Vegetable Risotto, 42
Vegetable Stock, 16
Vegetable Stuffed Peppers, 84
Vegetarian Tofu Stir-Fry, 76
Viking Vegetable Cassoulet, 74

W
Warm Mushroom Salad, 13
Wild Mushroom Sauce, 65
Winter Pear and Stilton Salad, 8

METRIC CONVERSION CHART

VOLUME MEASUREMENTS (dry)

1/8 teaspoon = 0.5 mL

1/4 teaspoon = 1 mL

1/2 teaspoon = 2 mL

3/4 teaspoon = 4 mL

1 teaspoon = 5 mL

1 tablespoon = 15 mL

2 tablespoons = 30 mL

1/4 cup = 60 mL

1/3 cup = 75 mL

1/2 cup = 125 mL

2/3 cup = 150 mL

3/4 cup = 175 mL

1 cup = 250 mL

2 cups = 1 pint = 500 mL

3 cups = 750 mL

4 cups = 1 quart = 1 L

VOLUME MEASUREMENTS (fluid)

1 fluid ounce (2 tablespoons) = 30 mL

4 fluid ounces (1/2 cup) = 125 mL

8 fluid ounces (1 cup) = 250 mL

12 fluid ounces (1 1/2 cups) = 375 mL

16 fluid ounces (2 cups) = 500 mL

WEIGHTS (mass)

1/2 ounce = 15 g

1 ounce = 30 g

3 ounces = 90 g

4 ounces = 120 g

8 ounces = 225 g

10 ounces = 285 g

12 ounces = 360 g

16 ounces = 1 pound = 450 g

DIMENSIONS

1/16 inch = 2 mm

1/8 inch = 3 mm

1/4 inch = 6 mm

1/2 inch = 1.5 cm

3/4 inch = 2 cm

1 inch = 2.5 cm

OVEN TEMPERATURES

250°F = 120°C

275°F = 140°C

300°F = 150°C

325°F = 160°C

350°F = 180°C

375°F = 190°C

400°F = 200°C

425°F = 220°C

450°F = 230°C

BAKING PAN SIZES

Utensil	Size in Inches/ Quarts	Metric Volume	Size in Centimeters
Baking or Cake Pan (square or rectangular)	8 × 8 × 2	2 L	20 × 20 × 5
	9 × 9 × 2	2.5 L	22 × 22 × 5
	12 × 8 × 2	3 L	30 × 20 × 5
	13 × 9 × 2	3.5 L	33 × 23 × 5
Loaf Pan	8 × 4 × 3	1.5 L	20 × 10 × 7
	9 × 5 × 3	2 L	23 × 13 × 7
Round Layer Cake Pan	8 × 1 1/2	1.2 L	20 × 4
	9 × 1 1/2	1.5 L	23 × 4
Pie Plate	8 × 1 1/4	750 mL	20 × 3
	9 × 1 1/4	1 L	23 × 3
Baking Dish or Casserole	1 quart	1 L	—
	1 1/2 quart	1.5 L	—
	2 quart	2 L	—